Unsettled Places

George Morgan is a senior lecturer at the
School of Humanities/Centre for Cultural Research,
University of Western Sydney.

Unsettled Places

Aboriginal People and Urbanisation in New South Wales

GEORGE MORGAN

Wakefield Press

For Butch and Brenda who lead by example

Wakefield Press
1 The Parade West
Kent Town
South Australia 5067
www.wakefieldpress.com.au

First published 2006

Cover designed by Liz Nicholson, designBITE
Text designed by Clinton Ellicott, Wakefield Press
Typeset by Ryan Paine, Wakefield Press
Printed and bound by Hyde Park Press

National Library of Australia
Cataloguing-in-publication entry

Morgan, George.
Unsettled places: Aboriginal people and urbanisation in New South Wales.
Bibliography.
Includes index.

ISBN-13: 978 1 86254 736 0 (pbk.).
ISBN-10: 1 86254 736 X (pbk.).

1. Aboriginal Australians – Cultural assimilation – New South Wales.
2. Aboriginal Australians – Urban residence – New South Wales.
3. Aboriginal Australians – New South Wales – Social conditions – 1788–1900.
4. Aboriginal Australians – New South Wales – Social conditions – 20th century.
5. Sacred space – New South Wales. I. Title.

303.42808999150944

Contents

Acknowledgments

This book has had a long gestation period and a number of people have helped to shape it. In the mid 1990s Ian Watson first told me of the New South Wales public housing tenancy files, and the Aboriginal records in particular, and suggested they might provide a fertile source for social history and historical sociology. These have been key sources. The staff of the New South Wales State Records Office in which the tenancy files are archived have been consistently helpful over a long period, in particular Indigenous archivist Kirsten Thorpe. (The New South Wales Department of Aboriginal Affairs funded a project to catalogue the personal/family information in the files to produce a database that will be helpful to Aboriginal people seeking to trace their families. The untiring commitment of research assistant Dianne Jarrett over several years was crucial to the completion of this database.)

Ken Johnston supervised the postgraduate research, on which this book is based. His wise counsel (and that of others listed below) is evident in the book's strengths, although the faults are, of course, all my own. While working at the University of Western Sydney's Goolangullia Aboriginal Education Centre between 1995 and 2001 I learned a great deal about urban Aboriginality. My colleagues – in particular Ann Flood, Terry Mason, Hyllus Munro, Joy Smith and Affrica Taylor – generously shared their ideas and discussed their life experiences with me. I learned much too from the numerous Indigenous students who enrolled in my classes in this period, many of whom come from families which had experienced urban transitions similar to those described in this book. Caroline Alcorso, Alistair Greig, Steve Kinnane, Clive Morgan, George Morgan (snr), Tim Rowse and Marie-Louise

Taylor provided invaluable comments on earlier drafts. Julia Beaven edited the manuscript in its later stages with great thoroughness.

In conversations over many years (and in their writings) my friends and colleagues Ghassan Hage, Raja Jayaraman, Greg Noble, and Scott Poynting have generously shared their ideas and enriched my understanding of contemporary colonialism, ethnicity and Australian nationalism. Emma Grahame taught me a long time ago that simplicity is the essence of clear writing. I am grateful to her for this insight and hope that my words are 'easy on the eye'. Each of my children – Rosa, Evan and Sam Morgan Grahame, and Natalie Marshall – have become young adults while I have been working on this book. Their vivaciousness has always inspired me.

In recent years my partner Cristina Rocha's enthusiasm for the twin vocations of research and writing, and her love and support, have inspired me to persevere with this project. Her book was published earlier this year and I am glad to be able to follow suit.

Introduction

Some years ago I attended a conference at which a Gandangarra leader welcomed delegates to his people's traditional lands. As he spoke I looked around at the formulaic interior of the lecture room and through the windows at a treeless, modernist streetscape of downtown Liverpool, part of Sydney's poor south-western suburbs. How incongruous it seemed. Here was a representative of one of the most ancient and distinctive cultures whose once flourishing, fertile country was now a Lego land of generic, concrete brutalism. We could have been anywhere in the world.

Few of us who live and work in Sydney are conscious on an everyday level of the colonial legacy. There are few memorials to those original people killed by epidemics or in the bloody conflicts over land and food sources in places which now form part of quiet suburban neighbourhoods. There is little to remind us that the bodies of black warriors were once displayed *in terrorem* in places where bungalows stand on quarter-acre lots. It is hard to imagine the fear that early colonisers experienced when the frontier was close at hand or their moral panic about the melding of civilisation and 'savagery'. All of this is erased from the collective memory. The modern city covers its tracks, denies its own conflictive prehistory. It acknowledges only those aspects of the past that accord with the narrative of progress towards the great, shining and consensual present.

The 1990s saw a great public outpouring of shame about the national past and the current plight of Aboriginal people. Hundreds of thousands of Australians signed sorry books, marched for land rights and attend Reconciliation events. How did this happen? Much has been written about the popular disenchantment with modernity, with the long-held verities of progress, growth and instrumental rationality with which Western (colonial) society is associated, and that shaped contemporary cities. The global environmental crisis has led many citizens of 'developed' nations to question the value and wisdom of their own culture, history and the actions of their governments. The search for alternatives has led many to embrace folk wisdom and new-age solutions. Indigenous culture and spirituality has been swept up in this and traditional motifs are now some of the central symbols of national identity.

These things are the cultural currency of Aboriginality yet they have less to do with the lives and culture of Aboriginal people in south-eastern Australia today than with the existential needs of non-Indigenous Australians for something primordial, something not tainted by modernity. In the past Australians were captivated by hairy-chested feats of pioneering endeavour: the legendary and heroic opening up of the county. This was a modernist narrative, the triumph of man over nature, in which Aboriginal people appeared as comic bit-part players – Jacky Jacky figures of fun. In recent history this has changed. Many in the West, disillusioned with modernity, romanticise the land and seek out the wisdom of its original custodians (Suzuki and Knudtson 1993). Ironically this has occurred at the point when most Aboriginal people live at some distance from their traditional land and are unable to practise ancient traditions and rituals.

This book looks at the ways Indigenous Australians came to live within the boundaries of towns and cities in New South Wales. This includes the resettlement and migration (if those words are not too strong) overseen by the state from the 1960s through government housing schemes. It also includes those who evaded the official spotlight by moving to inner-city or suburban housing before this time and who had thus, in the view of the Aborigines Welfare Board (AWB), relinquished their Aboriginality. For much of the twentieth century those living in rented housing in towns and cities had no official Indigenous status. To be a citizen (in the classical sense of the word) was to accept the obligation to assimilate.

Colonialism has made the places of Indigenous peoples in some senses strange and unfamiliar to them (Gelder and Jacobs 1998). The modernist development of these places – the reshaping of natural landscapes through agriculture and mining, the production of a built environment, and the imposition of the rhythms and movements of settlement – has obscured the sacred geographies, the narrative/spiritual emplacements of Aboriginality. Yet in parts of central and northern Australia, those areas most recently colonised, Indigenous sacred geographies are barely submerged (Merlan 1998). Where traditional owners remain on or close to their land, European and Indigenous spatial structures coexist uneasily and colonial erasure is never fully achieved.

However, colonialism has subjected the spaces of cities to more intensive physical and ideological work. In recent times community activists and academics, both Indigenous and non-Indigenous, have done much to peel back the layers and reveal the pre-colonial Aboriginal heritage in the Sydney basin (Attenbrow 2002; Turbet 1989; *see also* Hinckson 2001, whose guide to Aboriginal Sydney also covers recent history). The task of reconstructing an Indigenous geography in urban areas is much more formidable than is the case in less densely settled regions particularly, as in Sydney, where relatively few descendants of the original inhabitants remain (for a consideration of those of Darug descent *see* Kohen 1993). Although such reconstruction is important it is not the primary concern of this book.

Instead I will consider the state regulation of those who moved into rented housing in towns and cities and the way they responded to the cultural pressures they encountered. These people were neither the *tabula rasa* subjects of modernist social engineering nor for the most part were they traditional subjects. The Indigenous people of south-eastern Australia had experienced violence, displacement and assimilation long before they came to live within municipal boundaries. Brutal colonialism had shaped their identities as much as Aboriginal tradition. They struggled to sustain their solidarity and collective cultures in response to the efforts of the state to impose on them a conservative idea of suburban citizenship. But these cultures were to a large extent post-colonial. They were forged in adversity through engagement with European norms (Chapter 6 will deal with the complex question of urban Aboriginal identities). In short then, this book deals with the contemporary geography of colonialism, with the connections between urbanisation and assimilation, and with the forms of resistance offered by Aboriginal citizens.

When we whitefellas move away from our homelands it is generally to improve our life chances or to escape the gaze of 'communities' that stifle or restrict us. This is true of some Aboriginal people but historically most were displaced by coercion rather than choice. Many fled from racist persecution in the bush. Others confronted the dilemma which assimilation policies presented to them: live close to your family in a humpy on the reserve or apply for government housing in a suburban estate in a local town or distant city. To obtain modern housing you had to show yourself worthy of living as a respectable whitefella. If you traded community for a home you risked burning your bridges, being called a 'coconut', or an 'uptown black' by your people. Some evaded this difficult choice by heading for the black neighbourhoods of the inner cities. They left the bush in a process of chain migration that began in the 1940s, and went to live in houses crammed with relatives in places like Sydney's Redfern, and Fitzroy in Melbourne. Although many have moved frequently between city and bush, most have had connections to land and community weakened.

When Aboriginal people took up public housing they moved into an alien moral universe, a broad-acre monoculture of watchful neighbours and prying Housing Commission officials: *keep your front lawn mowed, hang curtains in your windows, don't let those relatives stay with you for too long, don't get drunk or have family arguments outside*. They faced a paradox. 'Real Aborigines', of course, lived in the outback. Those in the city were widely assumed to have jettisoned their culture and identity. On the other hand they were watched because they were Aboriginal. 'My uncle would always say', one woman told me, 'when you step out of your door try to look your best and behave well. Never give a white man anything to talk about'. Assimilation was a government policy but it was also a state of mind. It continued to blight the everyday lives of Aboriginal people long after the state formally adopted Indigenous self-determination.

Ironically urban and suburban places were in many ways more congenial to those who came to Australia from overseas. When my family migrated from England in the mid 1970s we did not think of ourselves as immigrants. We viewed Australia as an extension of our own country. The publicity films at Australia House in London had shown new suburban bungalows with happy Anglo families playing in neat backyards. These idyllic, middle-class visions entranced many Britons and continue to do so through television soap operas. We had little understanding of the history of colonialism which had made it possible for us to feel so much at home. Most Aboriginal people who moved to cities from reserves or camps on the banks of rivers underwent far greater cultural disorientation than did my family. Today the majority of Sydney-siders who identify as Indigenous live some distance from their home country in places built for them by whitefellas.

Colonialism has compromised Indigenous connections to the land. Most Aboriginal people who live in cities and towns cannot claim native title rights. Yet paradoxically most hold the symbols of ancient and traditional Aboriginal culture as their badges of identity. This is because even today most Australians assume that Aboriginality can only be a thread to the distant past, something essential and primordial. There are ways of being Aboriginal today that have nothing to do with bark paintings and dreaming stories. But it is difficult for Aboriginal people to say this: to say that culture is more than just the cultural commodities and spirituality, important though these may be; to say that it is the unswerving loyalty to family, the boisterous camaraderie, the boundless generosity; that it is also the pain of addiction, the emptiness of poverty and the grief of premature death. Some of this is private, not to be talked of with whitefellas. Much of it is not spoken of because for so long Aboriginal people have been taught that their culture is incompatible with the individualism and moral respectability of white society.

Most of us who live in Australia's densely inhabited spaces lose sight of people whose places and traditions are no longer their own but who continue to live and move amongst us. Under the banner of 'practical reconciliation' John Howard's government has shifted resources away from Aboriginal people in the cities and towards those living in rural and remote areas. The storm of protest and intense media attention around Indigenous rights in late nineties has subsided in the face of the continued electoral success of the Liberal National Coalition. Howard has restored the old hierarchy and mindset of the assimilation era where 'real Aborigines' live only in the bush. He has set about undermining the politics of self-determination under which Aboriginality was indivisible and inclusive.

A similar trend is evident in New South Wales where the state government is overseeing the redevelopment of Redfern, the symbolic heart of the Sydney Aboriginal community, on the fringes of the CBD. As we shall see in

Chapter 3, it was here in the 1960s and 70s that young Aboriginal people built a radical politics of self-determination to challenge paternalism and assimilationism, and a culture of pan-Aboriginality to build solidarity between Indigenous people from different parts of Australia. Today the Labor government's proposal to remove most Aboriginal housing in the area known as 'The Block' will allow the state and developers to realise the land values. But in the process the history of Aboriginal place-making in the area is being erased. Local residents will be dispersed leaving at best a cultural centre as a token gesture to mark their urban heritage. Such policies render problematic urban Indigenous identity claims.

The central task of this book is to consider the urbanisation of Aboriginal people in New South Wales from the mid-twentieth century, in particular those who moved into Housing Commission dwellings in urban areas from the 1960s. The early chapters trace the histories of the ideological, administrative and political structures that shaped this urbanisation. I am less concerned here with telling the stories of Indigenous people than with understanding how those who had colonised their land represented and regulated them in the period up to the 1960s. I consider the geographies of race, the production of urban space, and how the process of exclusion operated in the field of Aboriginal affairs. The social and political history of Aboriginal communities in this period has been written by historians more accomplished than myself (e.g. Goodall 1996). It is the later chapters that represent Aboriginal experiences more fully. Here I consider how they became urban and suburban subjects, and resisted, evaded and occasionally acquiesced to the assimilationist forces that bore down on them. In doing so I hope to have presented material that might help to illuminate contemporary urban Indigenous community, politics and culture.

Chapter 1 explores the reaction provoked by the presence of Indigenous people in and around nineteenth-century Sydney. The presence compromised the quest for genteel and orderly urban realm and the policies of Protection were partly designed to delineate the separate environments of coloniser and native.

Chapter 2 considers the politics of assimilation in country New South Wales in the middle decades of the twentieth century. This was a period in which the state through the New South Wales Aborigines Welfare Board (AWB) sought to secure cultural transformation of Aboriginal people. The vision of assimilation was one in which those on reserves, especially those deemed half-caste or of lesser Aboriginal blood, would eventually move into towns and become respectable citizens. This did not work both because of the racist intransigence of the residents of country towns and because most Indigenous people refused to identify with the vision that was offered to them and the loss of communal links this entailed. Many lived in circumstances of appalling poverty on overcrowded reserves or unofficial camps. Some fled these places and made for Sydney where in practical terms they were beyond the reach of the AWB.

Chapter 3 looks at the growth of Aboriginal communities in the city, how they were represented and how they spawned the pan-Aboriginal culture and the Black Rights movement that have been so influential since the 1970s.

Chapter 4 considers the suburban housing program that was introduced after the closure of the AWB at the end of the 1960s. In spite of the commitment of politicians to oversee the cultural acceptance and integration of Aboriginal people, they continued to experience, at the hands of housing officers, the sort of cultural shaming that was associated with reserve life and the assimilation regime.

Chapter 5 traces the lives of four Aboriginal people whose families moved to Sydney and its suburbs in the late 1960s. These case studies illustrate a range of responses to the social pressures they encountered from passing as white (hereafter the verb 'passing' will be used to describe this) to various strategies designed to sustain extended family/communal cultural ties.

Chapter 6 looks at how contemporary Indigenous culture and identity has been shaped by assimilation and urbanisation and considers how those who are living in modern settings relate to Aboriginal traditions.

Chapter 1

Colonial Geographies in Early New South Wales

The central focus of this book is the urbanisation of the New South Wales Aboriginal population from the mid-twentieth century. But in order to understand both how this process was regulated by the state and experienced by Aboriginal people themselves it is important to grasp the formation of early colonial space. The construction of settlements, towns and cities was not just a physical process. It involved the imposition of a moral order and a symbolic system on land. For much of Australian history the presence of Aboriginal people in towns and cities was incompatible with that order and system. Those who built camps in and around settlements compromised European pretensions to cultural superiority and signified the intrusion of wildness. They were widely perceived as 'fringe dwellers', completely demoralised and with neither the nobility of savagery nor the willingness to assimilate. This spectacle disturbed nineteenth-century observers and was partly responsible for the emergence of the discourses of Protection. 'Fringe dwellers' inhabited the ambiguous cultural spaces between Indigenous and European life and the central goal of native affairs was to remove them from this state of cultural limbo and thus clearly to demarcate the colonial from the native. This involved either, as in Protection, allowing Aboriginal people to recover a semblance of traditional life on government reserves or, as with later Assimilation policies, to oversee their transition to modern ways. The common symbolic geography of Protection and Assimilation associated Aboriginality only with nature/remote areas. Once Indigenous people entered towns and cities they were seen as remnants of their former traditional selves or in a process of becoming something else. Numerous writers have taken issue with this concept of Indigenous people as passive fringe dwellers and have discerned the cultural resilience and flexibility of those who had endured violence and deprivation to move into orbit of settlement in order to survive (Collman 1988; Goodall 1996; Sahlins 2000). Long before the state instigated a systematic Indigenous urban housing program, Indigenous people were adapting their cultures to the challenges posed by an implacable colonialism.

Settlement and the Production of Public Space

Throughout Australian history Aboriginal people have been inclined to cross an important symbolic line and come to live in European settlements despite the efforts, at various times, of white citizens and public authorities to exclude them. The early colonisers did not conceive of this journey as marking the transition from the rural to the urban, or from country to town. In south-eastern Australia in the late eighteenth and early nineteenth centuries colonial space was ordered according to different categories. Despite the fact that those who landed at Botany Bay in 1788 claimed vast territory for the Crown, colonial authorities classified land as settled or unsettled/wild. Unlike the English countryside the regions beyond the boundaries of towns were dangerous places. When frontier wars were being waged, those who lived close to the conflict demonised Indigenous people as savage and amoral. They feared attack and denied the humanity of their enemy. In the early 1800s the people of Sydney and its outposts were gripped with a siege mentality. The introduction of agriculture west and south west of Sydney had dispossessed Aboriginal people of their lands and food sources and resulted in violent encounters between farmers and traditional owners. This led governors King and later Macquarie (celebrated today as nation builder and visionary) to send out search and destroy missions against the Darug and Gandangarra (Goodall 1996).

In order to construct a town from the settlement it was necessary for colonial authorities to pacify the margins. European towns and cities were defined to a large extent by what surrounded them. Those who farmed the land not only supplied the townsfolk with food, they also practised, from a colonial viewpoint, a higher order of life than that of the hunter-gatherer. They provided the townsfolk with a buffer against the wilderness and all its dangers. In response to armed conflict Macquarie sought to generate stability by developing a radial road network around Sydney and assigning land grants along these routes. He was motivated by fear of the emergence of lawless vagabond settlements (members of which might consort with local Aboriginal people), much like the English forest communities who fed and sheltered highwaymen, than any rational calculated plan to decentralise the population. Parry points out that these roads were designed for the 'civilised rational man who travelled in a purposeful, directed way from a fixed establishment base' (Parry 1994). The spokes of 'civilisation' were cutting into what Macquarie saw as the potentially dangerous and lawless territory that girdled Sydney.

He also tried to conscript Aboriginal people to his vision of a hinterland populated by yeoman farmers. In 1819 Macquarie granted land to Colebee and Narragingy, partly as a reward for their assistance in punitive expeditions against Gandangarra, but also hoping these Darug men would become yeoman farmers and others might follow their example. Neither embraced this role. Colebee had little to do with the farm which was not on his traditional land and Narragingy, on whose land the grant was located, had only intermittent involvement, preferring to employ a European farm manager to run affairs (Brook and Kohen 1991, Chapter 3). Macquarie also established a native institution, first at Parramatta and later at Blacktown, in an (unsuccessful) attempt to assimilate the children of local Indigenous people (Brook and Cohen 1991).

Around this time some respectable, god-fearing residents of Sydney publicly voiced their disquiet at the spectacle of Aboriginal people in the streets of Sydney, many of whom were refugees from frontier wars. Many lamented the moral decline of the natives whose presence in Sydney served to undermine the quest for a cultured and orderly public domain. The *Sydney Gazette*–an early organ of colonial public opinion–expressed alarm at the ways in which Aboriginal people fought each other in city streets to the amusement of white onlookers. They were:

> disposed at moments of intemperance to hack and hew one another all to pieces, mostly for the purpose of affording sport to their [European] spectators . . . and did we perceive amongst this poor and supine set of people that they possessed a natural inclination to destroy each other, why then we might reasonably reconcile ourselves to their feats of

depopulation; but this is so far from being the case that they are known to be friendly to each other in the bush ... For many years they gave a preference to Sydney for the display of prowess, and perhaps no engagement ever here took place but under circumstances of inebriation (*Sydney Gazette* 31 October 1818).

Captain Bellinghausen, in command of a Russian ship that visited Sydney in 1820 on a scientific voyage, wrote that he found it deplorable that the Aboriginal people in the town 'should have taken over from the convicts all the imprecations, oaths and curses of the English rabble'. He went on to say that fighting amongst themselves was 'a daily and even hourly occurrence' (Debenham 1945, p. 329). This continued into the 1830s with frequent reports in the Sydney newspapers of Aboriginal street violence from 1837–1839 (Reece 1974, p. 9).

It is important to question the ways in which colonial commentators described and accounted for the public violence in urban areas. The common assumption that once Aboriginal people were in the town, removed from the bush environment, they were involved only in individualised violence which was unconnected to traditional law or tribal rivalries, is almost certainly erroneous. Brook and Cohen note that organised warfare between tribal groups took place in the regions around Sydney well into the nineteenth century (Brook and Cohen 1991, p. 98). The mixing of different groups in the streets of the town was a recipe for continued prosecution of pre-existing conflicts. In a contemporary anthropological study of the fighting habits of Wiradjuri men in country towns, MacDonald argues against viewing such violence as indicating a complete demoralisation of Aboriginal culture (McDonald 1988). Rather, it is tied up, she claims, with traditional culture and ritual.

Many of those who observed Sydney in the 1820s were shocked at the spectacle of Indigenous destitution. Anglo-American artist Augustus Earle, for example, lived in the town for two years in the middle of the decade. His paintings and sketches of Aboriginal people show them as demoralised fringe dwellers. The works say as much about the prejudices of the painter as they do about the situation of those he represents. A famous image of George Street from 1825 (*see* Figure 1), for example, shows a

Figure 1

group sitting in the street with no apparent purpose, some dressed in the cast-off clothing of whites and with bottles and clubs. They are represented doing things in public – sitting, eating, drinking – that, according to colonial morality, should be performed in private. This has been an enduring way of framing and disparaging Aboriginality. White society is represented strolling purposefully in the background. Earle wrote of native people that 'they have neither energy, enterprise, nor industry; and their curiosity can scarcely be excited' (Earle 1832, p. 259). In 1839 the *Australian* reported that a group of Aboriginal people was arrested for being drunk and fighting outside the Hyde Park Barracks 'dancing their native dances and disturbing the whole neighbourhood' (Reece 1974, p. 10).

While these words and images embodied the views of many colonists who saw Aboriginal people as a savage, inferior race, from the late 1820s there was a countervailing tendency. Progressive colonists were alarmed by the reports of violent treatment of Aboriginal people in remote areas and called for their protection. Those who had campaigned for the abolition of slavery elsewhere in the colonised world, many of them Evangelical Christians, turned their attention to frontier New South Wales where squatters grabbed land and murdered its owners openly with impunity. The prosecution of some of those responsible for murdering Aboriginal people at Myall Creek in 1838 at the behest of reformist Governor Gipps was symptomatic of a softening of colonial policy.

Many protectionists romanticised pre-invasion Indigenous society in a way that has become more prevalent in recent times. This romantic conception had its origins in Enlightenment thinking. French philosopher Jean Jacques Rousseau popularised the archetype of the noble savage. He argued that modernity brings overpopulation, scarcity, competition and oppressive governance. For Rousseau those living in a 'primitive' state exist instinctively, cooperatively and at one with nature free from the enslavements of oppressive labour. In modern society our natural instincts are dulled and we become cerebral, competitive and egotistical. In describing the passage from savagery to modernity Rousseau presents a secular version of the Biblical myth of the Fall of Man. Indigenous people living in a traditional manner represent a remnant of this earlier state. They are uncorrupted by the greed and alienation of the West. When exposed to the forces of modern life they are overwhelmed and quickly lose their cultural bearings. Such perspectives continue to influence popular perceptions of Indigenous peoples including those living in urban areas today.

In the second half of the nineteenth century, government reserves set up in New South Wales afforded Aboriginal people some protection. Goodall (1996) has explored the key role Indigenous people played in supporting the establishment of reserves so that they could obtain some control over at least some fragments of land and culture. However many remained in the densely settled areas, a reminder of the legacy of early settlement. An editorial of the *Illustrated Sydney News* drew a stark and pathetic picture of those in colonial cities and their 'noble' forebears:

> The miserable being occasionally seen in our cities and country towns prematurely aged and decrepit by the vices of intemperance is by no means to be taken as a type of the once brave and warlike aboriginal of Australia. In his savage state he had a code of morality and a rigorous

> system of customs and laws ... which hedged him in and preserved law and order in each tribe and which the white man has broken down without substituting anything better (17 February 1883).

Reserves were established on land away from white settlements that was generally poor and not really suitable for agriculture and grazing. Here Aboriginal people were expected to regenerate their roots and rediscover their traditions. They also served as places to which fringe dwellers could be taken away from the delicate eyes of those in the cities and towns, most of whom, hostile or sympathetic to Aboriginal people, were anxious to secure the lines of cultural division between themselves and the native other. Protection was based partly on humanitarian sentiment but also on a sense of cultural insecurity that is characteristic of settler societies.

In this period many administrators and public commentators believed the Aboriginal race was doomed but that the policies of Protection would bestow dignity upon them and 'smooth the dying pillow' (McGregor 1997). In 1880 the *Bulletin* newspaper, which became an expression of emergent radical nationalism, published an editorial that contained a premature epitaph for the Indigenous Australians:

> The Australian Aborigine is a doomed man. The 'civilised black' as we in New South Wales know him, is a wretched creature. He is madly fond of drink. His future was blasted before his birth by the vices of white man ... Drunkenness and degradation are at all times pitiable sights; but just as they are the more terrible when associated with the painted faces, the grating blasphemy, the vulgar tawdriness which too often characterises unfortunates of our own race, so the Aborigines appearance, as he wanders along the streets which were once his hunting grounds, is lent an additional melancholy by the tattered finery in which he is arrayed ... It is too late to talk about preserving the Aboriginal race. It is and always was utopian to try and Christianise it. Rum and European clothes have ruined the people who, half a century ago, were temperate and naked. The Aboriginal race is moribund. All we can now do is to give an opiate to the dying man, and, when he expires, bury him respectably (19 June 1880, p. 1).

Protection and Dispersal

At the end of the nineteenth century there were increasingly insistent calls for the removal of Indigenous people from the streets of Sydney. The city's population had grown from 54,000 in 1851 to 96,000 in 1861 and 383,000 by 1891 and there were widespread fears among the middle classes about the threats that were posed by the urban masses (Wotherspoon 1983, p. 15). The camps of Indigenous people in and around the city were seen as a source of moral danger, as magnets to dissolute white men – places for sly grog and illicit sexual activity. There were moves to close them down. For example, a Mr Henson (Member for Canterbury) reported to New South Wales parliament in 1886 that there was a camp of 'about thirty Aborigines' at Lavender Bay near Sydney. He said he 'need not point out the undesirable state of things that might result from the existence of a native encampment in such close proximity to the city' and that 'scenes of a disgraceful character had already occurred there and . . . steps should be taken to prevent these people becoming a nuisance and a disgrace to society'.[1] Around this time small groups of Indigenous people were arriving in Sydney from the Illawarra, the Burragorang Valley and the Hunter River as a result of the sufferings which they were experiencing on their lands (Goodall 1996, p. 89). Those from the Illawarra were camping at La Perouse and many of the others took up residence in the boatsheds at Circular Quay.

The presence of these people partly explained the decision by the New South Wales government of Henry Parkes to appoint George Thornton as Protector of Aborigines, to empower him to inquire into Indigenous living conditions in the colony and to recommend what action might be taken in the future. Thornton found a need to expand the reserve network but also to establish a system of indoor or institutional relief. The subsequent establishment of the Aborigines Protection Board (APB) marked a shift from the more hands-off approach, which had prevailed to that point, towards a policy of tighter moral control over Aboriginal communities through the establishment of institutions and institutional regulation of Indigenous populations. The new Board acquired the power to appoint managers to government stations, to remove children from families in situations where they deemed that neglect was occurring and to determine who had the right to live on particular reserves. The institutionalisation of Aboriginal people from the late nineteenth century paralleled the changes which had earlier been adopted in Britain to provide support for the poor (Long 1970). The British New Poor Law of 1834 had replaced the established system of outdoor relief with one where those without other means of support–particularly the urban poor–were removed from the streets and placed in workhouses. In moving in this direction government reserves and stations became more institutional in character. As in Britain, this process occurred in New South Wales during a period of rapid urban growth.

Many reserves were located well away from the white population. Some, however, like La Perouse established with a small population in the 1880s on Sydney's southern outskirts, were too close for the comfort of many residents. The expansion of the city's population and boundaries to the south created a situation that alarmed administrators of Aboriginal affairs. A process of chain migration of Aboriginal people from the south coast had increased the size of the La Perouse population from the original 100 or so, to several hundred. As Sydney's tramline network was extended to the vicinity of the reserve, the Protection Board adopted more coercive measures to deal with this perceived problem. The annual report of 1903 stated:

> There are still a large number of aborigines resident on the Reserve at La Perouse. In order to keep visitors to Botany Bay off the reserve it was suggested that a higher boundary fence should be erected round it ... The police were requested to continue their efforts to induce the aborigines there to go back to their native districts, but, notwithstanding all efforts to keep down the numbers, visitors are constantly arriving from the country.
>
> Owing to the bad behaviour of some of those at the camp when travelling to and from Sydney, the Railway Commissioners found it necessary to withdraw the privilege from the aborigines for riding free on the trams.[2]

Ration and blanket allocations were withdrawn from those who were not official residents. Many of those deemed to be outsiders were expelled and transported to remote parts of the state, often to the government station at Warangesda. These measures had little effect. Many returned and eventually an unofficial settlement known as Frog Hollow grew up alongside the official reserve. There were several attempts in the early twentieth century to close down the reserve completely but resistance from both the Aboriginal residents and liberal Europeans ensured that these were unsuccessful. As we shall see in the next chapter, elsewhere in New South Wales similar conflicts early in the twentieth century produced less favourable outcomes for Aboriginal people.

Also in this period it became apparent that a central premise of Protection Policy – that the Aboriginal race was in decline and would eventually die out – was mistaken. The Indigenous population was increasing by World War One (McIntyre 1999, pp. 144–145). The Board became more energetic in its efforts to separate those deemed half-caste or of lesser blood from full bloods. The assumption that the former group would willingly break links with the latter was misplaced. This drove the Board to increasingly coercive action in pursuit of the desired result: children were taken from parents in greater numbers and families were 'relocated' away from reserves. As Goodall observed:

> The Protection Board had aimed to make Aboriginal people disappear culturally and socially to become atomised, nuclear families of working class Australians. Instead it succeeded only in a conjurer's sleight of hand, in which they disappeared from one locality only to resettle close by, no longer on the [Aborigines Protection Board] rations list but still identifying with their own lands and communities. These new living areas were often the camps outside towns in the district . . . (Goodall 1996, p. 173).

Post-colonialism and the Narrative of the Fall

The history of Aboriginal affairs has been based on the desire to extract Aboriginal people from this state of stalled transition between tradition and modernity. This has involved a range of strategies. Protection and Assimilation were key regimes of colonial governance and have been part of a repertoire of ideological responses to the 'Indigenous problem'. Elements of this repertoire emerge at key moments. Protection, for example, has enduring ideological influence even though it has long disappeared as a formal policy. It continues to shape certain contemporary perspectives on Indigenous cultural heritage and often frames debates on how to address the problems of remote area communities.

Protection is informed by a narrative structure – the narrative of the fall – that leads us to think of Indigenous people in certain ways and the elements of which we can plot. Firstly, prior to colonisation they had a way of life (wise or backward depending on your point of view) that was timeless and primordial. 'History' arrived with the colonisers (Healey 1997). Secondly, as we have observed, this arrival drew them into an inexorable cycle of decline. They were swept up by the colonial juggernaut and remained unable to make history or shape their destinies in any way. Thirdly the narrative implies that not only are they deprived of the ability to make history but that they lose the ability to create communal culture and sustain Indigenous identity. They become fringe dwellers, pathetic remnants of their former selves, swept up by unassailable forces (Clifford 1988, p. 5).

The narrative of the fall encourages a view of Indigenous people as passive, powerless and child-like. To be good to them is to act paternalistically towards them. In protectionist terms this means to guard them against the onslaughts of modernity. In assimilationist terms it entails guiding them gently into a conventional white way of life. There is no place in this ideology to conceive of Aboriginal people actively sustaining their Indigenous identities while inhabiting the ambiguous and 'in-between' cultural and social spaces of settler society. The more distant they are from a traditional lifestyle, the more their Aboriginality is depleted. Those who dwell in or around towns and cities *ipso facto* suffer such depletion.

But transactions between coloniser and colonised are never conducted exclusively on the terms of the former (Thomas 1991). Sahlins takes issue with the view of colonialism as a cultural juggernaut, destroying all in its wake, arguing that Indigenous people have a great capacity for cultural recuperation (Sahlins 2000). This is illustrated in the ways they shaped European rituals around their own traditions. For example, when church missionaries tried to establish camps and festivities at Christmas time to promote their faith, Aboriginal people, rather than resisting completely, organised their own celebrations at Christmas time at traditional meeting places away from the European settlements or missions (Byrne 1996). Cultural mixing and innovation were also apparent in the ways in which Indigenous people used European commodities. Byrne observes that they adapted blankets as slings to carry babies and that while they wore trousers, dresses and jackets to curry favour with the invaders, hats and scarves were 'objects of direct or unmediated desire' (Byrne 1996 p. 83). Such evidence challenges the idea that colonialism always involves a brittle encounter: on the one side, formidable imperialism, on the other, fragile, yielding Indigenous culture. Cultures are not fixed, bounded and discrete as is suggested in the tradition of hermeneutic philosophy, but are constantly in dialogue (Bakhtin 1994).

In colonial/Indigenous interactions each made sense of the other through their pre-existing structures of language and culture. Rowse, for example, in his study of rationing in central Australia wrote of the need to recognise that Aboriginal people interpreted the allocation of food, blankets and other rations through their own traditions of reciprocity (Rowse 1998). The acceptance of rations did not mark a point of irrevocable absorption into the Western economic system and symbolic realm. The transaction had a social significance for Aboriginal people very different to that for Europeans. Historians and anthropologists have also cited numerous Indigenous influences on settler culture, particularly in remote areas (Reynolds 1990; Hamilton 1990). The dealings between native peoples and colonisers involved a process of adaptation and cultural construction on both sides of the frontier.

The issue of reciprocal cultural influence has preoccupied post-colonialist theorists, many of whom argue that colonising powers have been unable to keep Indigenous people and their culture at arm's length, separated from the imperial centres, or to effectively assimilate those people (Rattansi 1997). Colonisation produces a field of hybrid cultural expression which is neither entirely colonial nor Indigenous in a traditional sense (Bhabha 1985). Colonised peoples disrupt the pretensions of those who invade their lands. Those who live on the fringes of settlement can prove to be a thorn in the side of the colonisers holding them up to derision through parody and irony.

There is certainly evidence of an irreverent Indigenous presence in nineteenth-century Sydney. Some Aboriginal people were skilful mimics and clowns and engaged in public behaviour designed to lampoon the formality and stiffness of the colonial gentry. Surgeon Peter Cunningham wrote of a ball at Captain Piper's mansion where an Aboriginal man mocked a pretentious guest:

> What should present itself at his very elbow but a sort of goblin facsimile of his own person, in every particular except that of a white face, skimming round and round, in exact imitative concord with his own manner and movements (Cunningham 1966).[3]

Barron Field who travelled to New South Wales to become a judge, wrote of the Aboriginal people of 1820s Sydney that they '... have a bowing acquaintance with everybody, and scatter their How-d'ye-dos with an air of friendliness and equality, and with a perfect English accent' (Field 1825, p. 436). Later in the century an editorial in the *Bulletin* described the typical Aboriginal inhabitant of Sydney thus:

> The poor inebriated wretch struts along George Street, imitating with the pantomimic ability which is one of his few mental gifts, the deliberate gait of the policeman who once wore the rags which cover his back, or the stilted walk of the volunteer who has given him a cast off hat (*Bulletin* 19 June 1880, p. 1).

Wearing tattered finery they had procured from charitable passers by, these people had much in common with the Larrikin folk devils of the late nineteenth-century Australian cities (Morgan 1997). They would loiter in the streets, insulting the promenading gentlefolk, publicly confronting colonial stiffness and formality.

The Indigenous presence on the fringe is unsettling. Where native people can be conserved in noble savagery – barbaric, heathen, instinctive, primitive – then they provide an ethnological counterpoint, confirming our moral and intellectual superiority. Where they come to inhabit the symbolic world of the colonisers, albeit as insider-outsiders, they disrupt our complacent and imperious claims to moral, intellectual and cultural superiority. As Byrne argues '[t]he native Other became a dimension of the European subject ... White Australia became locked into maintaining its construction of the traditional static Aborigine partly because the stability of its own identity depended upon it' (Byrne p. 91).

Conclusion

In this chapter I have considered the representations of Aboriginal people in colonial Sydney and the governance structures that emerged to deal with the 'native problem'. Although the twentieth-century Indigenous urban journeys were mostly made under quite different circumstances, it is important to understand the colonial construction of urban space and the cultural categories that were used to make sense of the presence of Aboriginal people. In establishing the places that became the towns and cities of Australia, the European colonisers imposed a system of organising land that was alien to Indigenous people. They constructed houses, streets and public buildings. They divided space into public and private. They forged enclaves of 'civilised' settlement on the traditional lands of hunter-gatherers both through symbolic and physical labour. The exclusion of all disturbing traces of Aboriginality was central to the process of settlement, to the eventual production of the urban realm in Australia. From the 1820s the presence of Aboriginal people in the streets of Sydney appeared incongruous and anachronistic. It signified their impending cultural and physical demise and prompted calls for their exclusion and protection on reserves. The narrative of the fall represented Indigenous people on the fringes of settlements as passive, silent and demoralised, unable to shape their destinies in any way. It underpinned Protection and Assimilation and imposed upon the state an obligation to move Indigenous people in one direction or the other: towards the lifestyles and places of tradition or those of modernity. This perspective failed to acknowledge the agency of those people. Their presence on the fringe, far from signifying cultural attrition, was evidence of their resourcefulness as they struggled to survive in the wake of dispossession and cultural genocide. The next chapter deals with Assimilation policies and how they were spatialised. It will look at how the state managed the relationship between Aboriginal people and cities both in broad policy terms and in terms of the micro-management of everyday life.

Chapter 2

Uplifting Fantasies: Modernism and the Quest for Aboriginal Advancement

In 1937 Australian governments formally adopted the policy of Assimilation. The Indigenous social order had endured despite the prophecy that the Aboriginal race was doomed and despite measures designed to fulfil that prophecy such as the removal of children from parents and their placement in children's homes.[1] Assimilation was a response to the recognition that the numbers of those identifying as Indigenous (and recognised as such in the bush) were increasing in spite of the efforts in the early twentieth century to disperse them into the white working class (Goodall 1995). Assimilation also reflected the growing influence of modernism in the activities of the state and the official ambition to transform those with residual minority cultural affiliations, including Indigenous people, into respectable individualised suburban citizens. Assimilation committed the state to securing the 'advancement' of Aboriginal people rather than overseeing their demise.

This fundamentally changed the nature of reserves[2] and their relationship to nearby towns and cities. In New South Wales, they became sites of confinement and social engineering in which the officers of the (euphemistically named) Aborigines Welfare Board (formed in 1940 to replace the APB) disparaged Aboriginal language, culture and traditions and promoted nuclear family life, wage labour and the moral economy of white Australia. Those inclined to embrace this new way of life could seek to be formally exempt from Board control and abandon the reserve to go to live in town with the (largely illusory) benefits of improved material security and enhanced citizen rights. In this era the municipal boundaries marked the threshold between the old life and the new for Aboriginal people. The AWB required those who sought exemption to burn their bridges. But whatever the express official intentions, the conservative establishments in country towns continued to resist the resettlement schemes as they had effectively during the period when the APB applied the policies of dispersal. Townspeople fiercely resisted the intrusion of Aboriginality and had little time for the official narratives of assimilation.

As reserves were closed or diminished in size under the pressure of agricultural development so the numbers of those living in unofficial camps, usually in poor, flood-prone areas increased dramatically. By the early 1960s there was a crisis in the Aboriginal affairs in New South Wales with the AWB unable to resolve the contradictions it faced, and most Aboriginal people living in conditions of appalling poverty and social marginalisation. This chapter will trace the circumstances that led the New South Wales government to close the AWB in 1969, to allocate responsibility for most Aboriginal matters to mainstream government departments, and systematically to integrate Aboriginal people into residential areas of large towns and cities.[3]

Modernism, Assimilation and the New Deal

During the middle third of the twentieth century, Assimilation was the central ideology of colonialism. Paul Hasluck, Commonwealth Minister for Aboriginal Affairs from 1951–1963 wrote: 'We Australians ... have a vast repair job to do on the wreckage of a people, rather than a messianic role of leading them back into the wilderness to dwell apart forever' (Hasluck 1998, p. 149). In this period concerned citizens used a new vocabulary when referring to Indigenous people. Rather than calling for Protection they appealed for Aboriginal 'advancement', 'progress' or 'uplift'. If we could not recreate the traditional environment then at least we could give them a leg-up: pluck them from cultural limbo and guide them towards respectability and encourage nuclear family life, regular jobs, conventional gender roles, sobriety and moral rectitude. The implementation of Assimilation policies by the state did not, however, match the altruistic rhetoric of well-meaning (though paternalistic) pressure groups.

Modernism had a powerful influence on government, administration and public opinion in Australia as elsewhere the world. It was characterised by a faith in the ability of humankind to triumph over nature, and of experts, planners and technicians to wipe away the encumbrances of traditions, to dispel social conflict, and to construct an orderly and harmonious society. Aspects of modernist discourse had emerged in the nineteenth century in fields of professional practice but at this time the state had played only a night-watch role, intervening very little in the social and economic lives of its citizens beyond the imposition of law and order. It was only with the expansion of the state in the twentieth century – in welfare, social regulation and administration – that modernism solidified into institutional political form.

Modernist regimes enlisted experts of all sorts. Scientists, planners, bureaucrats, doctors and others devoted their energies to clearing up the messy and dissonant aspects of the past and designing and realising a world of pure functionality and conformity. Many such experts became enormously powerful social engineers with scant regard for civil liberties and they tolerated little resistance. Those who suffered included ethnic minorities, the 'undeserving' poor, and other groups who authorities believed posed a threat to social order and cultural convention. This was an era of professional zealotry. Those charged with pursuing the modernist vision often lost sight of the humanity of those who were subject to their 'reforms'. Their visions and projects were teleological, only acknowledging those aspects of the past that were in harmony with their synthetic futures.

Modernist social policy was designed to direct minority groups towards cultural conformity and respectable habits. In Australia, the White Australia Policy favoured the immigration of those deemed more able to assimilate. The state expected migrants to abandon homeland traditions and embrace the national way of life. The methods used to achieve assimilation in Aboriginal affairs were far more barbaric and coercive than any encountered by immigrants. The removal of children and the forced displacement away from traditional lands were two such methods. The stories of many of these children, most of whom in New South Wales were placed in institutions at Cootamundra and Kinchella, were documented in heart-rending terms in the Human Rights and Equal Opportunity Commission report *Bringing them Home* that provoked enormous public sympathy in the late nineties (HREOC 1996).

Those who lived on government reserves were taught to be ashamed of their culture. The AWB staff forbade them to speak their language, discouraged the staging of ceremonies and did all they could to prevent elders influencing young people. Reserve dwellers had to endure regular inspections of their homes as officials imposed standards of hygiene, moral probity and domestic order. The humiliation associated with such inspections left lasting scars on many, particularly women. Those who wished to escape state regulation could apply to be exempt from the provisions of Aboriginal welfare legislation but had to undertake to become estranged from those who remained under the Board's control. So Aboriginal people were given an invidious choice. They could remain poor and under state regulation or secure more citizenship rights (and potentially economic benefits) if they were prepared to surrender communal ties. Few did so. Between 1943 and 1964 only 1500 out of a possible 14,000 applied for exemption (Goodall 1995, p. 90).

The first official public expression of Assimilation Policy emerged from a gathering of administrators and ministers for Aboriginal affairs in the national capital in 1937. They resolved that 'the destiny of the natives of aboriginal origin, but not of the full bloods, lies in their ultimate absorption by the people of the Commonwealth'. Although this was only a commitment to 'biological absorption' very soon the Commonwealth Government came to recognise that there was little hope that Aboriginality would simply be bred out (Gray 1998, p. 57). Those with Aboriginal blood would have to undergo social and cultural transformation. This changed approach came in the context of an upsurge in Aboriginal activism in south-eastern Australia during the 1930s. Around this time Aboriginal rights campaigners like William Ferguson and Jackie Patten, leaders of the Aborigines Progressive Association, organised protests against the conditions prevailing on reserves.

The organisation demanded both civil rights and material security for all Aboriginal people. In keeping with the era it sought a transition to modernity but failed to anticipate the social and cultural trauma that this transition would involve. It aimed to 'raise all Aborigines throughout the Commonwealth to full citizenship status and civil equality with whites' (*Australian Abo Call* April 1938, p. 1). APA activists argued that this involved equal access to labour protection, health care, housing and land ownership rights, education and social security:

> In regard to uncivilised and semi-civilised Aborigines, we suggest that patrol officers, nurses and teachers, both men and women, of **Aboriginal blood** should be specially trained by the Commonwealth government as Aboriginal Officers to bring the wild people into contact with civilisation (p. 1, their emphasis).

In the late 1930s the Commonwealth Government announced a 'New Deal' for Aboriginal people. Minister for the Interior John McEwen proclaimed this would 'entitle them by right and by qualification to the ordinary rights of citizenship' and 'encourage them to move away from traditional nomadic inclinations to a settled life' (Gray 1998, p. 56). The government had relied on the advice of anthropologist AP Elkin of the University of Sydney, a formidable advocate for assimilation in the post-war decades. The impetus for this New Deal was lost after the outbreak of World War Two

During World War Two the federal government became involved in the social and economic life of the nation as never before – organising wartime production, commandeering industrial facilities, regulating labour on the home front as well as supplying troops to various theatres of conflict. The impetus of the 'command' state carried through to the period of post-war reconstruction. Town planning and housing were central to this reconstruction. The Commonwealth/State Housing Agreement of 1945 led to the formation of housing authorities in each of the states. These bodies set out to provide suburban 'homes fit for heroes', (public housing for low-income families). The post-war decades saw vast numbers of young people, the parents of the baby-boom generation, decanted from the confines of the inner city, where they had been renting cramped flats or rooms in the houses of relatives, to the new urban fringe estates. A home in the outer suburbs came to symbolise idyllic family life.

For a brief period senior academics and public servants debated the question of whether Aboriginal people might move from reserves and camps into towns and cities, and if so, how this might be managed. The Commonwealth Housing Commission report had stated that 'a dwelling of good standard and equipment is not only the need but the right of every citizen' (cited in Greig 1995, p. 32). However, this pledge was never intended to apply to Aboriginal people who were not considered to be citizens.[4] Hasluck, who as federal minister had little power over Indigenous people except those in the Northern Territory, observed there was no comprehensive plan for native affairs in the post-war years (Hasluck 1988, p. 74).

The Western Australian government wrote to the Minister for Post-War Reconstruction in 1944 seeking advice on the matter of Aboriginal housing. In response, Director of the Department HC Coombs wrote a series of letters casting around for information and opinions from various public servants and experts in other states on housing and assimilation. He wrote:

> One problem raised by Western Australia concerns those natives who are living under completely civilised conditions and who are workers within the full meaning of the term in accordance with white standards of life. It is possible that many of these may make application for the erection of homes away from native reservations and amidst or contiguous to homes which the Western Australian government proposes to erect for white workers. Since most white people do not approve of the near residence of coloured people it seems probable that there will be difficulties on racial grounds.[5]

At the time most Aboriginal residents of government reserves and unofficial camps in New South Wales lived in dreadful housing that lacked bathrooms, proper kitchens or internal power or water. The Director of Postwar Reconstruction in New South Wales (presumably in consultation with the AWB), A Max Allen, described plans to establish 'three or four new stations which will be laid out on the lines of model village settlements having the amenities and facilities of modern life'. These were to be situated away from the popular residential areas of any town. In developing these stations, at Murrin Bridge for example, the New South Wales government intended to close down a number of smaller reserves and relocate the residents. The letter stated a commitment to encouraging the 'better type of Aboriginal' to take up residence in small towns and to 'clean up some of the undesirable camps'. There was, however, no recognition of the barriers which Indigenous people faced in their quest to move into town housing, something which the AWB was never able to overcome.

Most significant was the advice of Elkin, then a member of the AWB, furnished in a letter dated 20 November 1944. It reflects his belief, stated in his book *Citizenship for Aborigines*, published in the same year, that the state should carefully manage the transition of Indigenous people from 'nomadism' to full citizenship through a process of staged assimilation (Elkin 1944). He expressed scepticism that the process of assimilation could be achieved through housing Aboriginal nuclear families individually in white neighbourhoods 'unless the person concerned is light in colour and married to a white person, he should not be encouraged to live with his wife and children as an isolated unit in the midst of the white community'. He observed that there was a stigma attached to marriage between white women and Indigenous men, but not vice versa: 'a white man lifts a woman up to the white status; on the other hand, a white woman tends to slip from her status when married to a half caste'. His preference was for 'mixed bloods' to live in groups so they might enjoy the benefits of mutual support, rather than being scattered throughout residential areas.[6]

He went on to say that if Aboriginal people are to be housed in town areas they should be situated in the 'intermediate section of town, and not in the slum parts or among the "toffs"'. This was consistent with the schemes that town planning schemes and social engineers had for the 'deserving poor' at the time: they would become respectable citizens if removed from the degrading slum environments in which they were forced to live as a result of the shortage of good housing. Elkin argued that Aboriginal people seeking to move away from the reserves and camps 'are presumably good workers and our own working class people do not really object to them'. However, in concluding his letter to Coombs, Elkin said he shared the reluctance of the New South Wales Board for rapid assimilation: 'We cannot hurry the scheme as fast as we would like. The psychological and sociological problems are very great.'

Little resulted from the process of consultation undertaken by Coombs. Hasluck characterises the post-war period as one in which Aboriginal 'advancement' proved something of a hot potato, with neither the states nor the Commonwealth prepared to take the lead (Hasluck 1988, pp. 74–78). In 1944 the Australian people had had the chance to vote on the transference of powers from the states to the Commonwealth in various areas including Aboriginal affairs. This was defeated largely because of strong opposition to the granting of power in some other areas. The states, therefore, retained constitutional responsibility for Aboriginal affairs until a later referendum held in 1967, but were reluctant to undertake measures of social and economic improvement without special Commonwealth funding assistance. This was not forthcoming. None of the post-war governments of the forties and fifties treated the issues as of high priority. The impetus for change which had been generated in the late 1930s was not recovered until the mid 1960s.

Dawn Magazine, Reserves and Domestic Tutelage

In the 20 years after World War Two, Aboriginal people on reserves were subjected to great pressures to embrace standards of hygiene, 'domestic pride', family life and work habits 'appropriate' for suburban life. Government officials sought to inculcate shame in relation to traditional Indigenous culture. It is quite common for young Aboriginal people today to express regret at the reluctance of their grandparents to pass on the culture–to speak the language and to relay dreaming stories and other traditional knowledge to their descendants.[7] This may in some cases be because the elders do not trust the young people, many of who have moved away from their homelands, to respect and nurture those traditions. More often, however, it demonstrates the legacy of cultural shaming practices.

The assimilationist strategies of the AWB were best illustrated in its magazine *Dawn* that appeared between 1952 and 1975. The journal was ostensibly intended to teach Indigenous people about the habits of life that would guarantee their acceptance into society. The cover design exemplifies the ideology of cultural improvement. The masthead (*see* Figure 2), situated on the left of the page, is made up of a man of classically Aboriginal features gazing into the middle distance in noble savage fashion. On the opposite side, separated by the word *Dawn* (from which rays of sunshine emanate), is a graphic of a cityscape. This signifies both a transition from primitiveness to modernity and from ignorance to enlightenment. The chair of the AWB, C J Buttsworth, wrote in the April 1953 edition:

> Aboriginal people would become completely assimilated if they adopted habits and standards of living similar to those of the white community ... one of the main differences at present is the poor type of housing so many Aboriginal people provide for themselves. It has been said that his home is an Englishman's castle. This is true not only of Englishmen but of all civilised people. Home is the cornerstone of our

Volume No. 4
Ser. No. 8
Dawn
A MAGAZINE FOR THE ABORIGINAL PEOPLE OF N.S.W.
AUGUST, 195

Figure 2

Volume No. 5
Ser. No. 12
Dawn
A MAGAZINE FOR THE ABORIGINAL PEOPLE OF N.S.W.
DECEMBER, 19
Merry Christmas
1955

Figure 3

existence and there should be the strongest urge within all people to make their homes comfortable and beautiful happy places in which to live with their families, places to be kept clean and tidy and to be made pretty with paints and flowers (p. 1).

This lament captures the central ideological ambition informing Aboriginal affairs in the second half of the twentieth century: to domesticate those whose forebears had led wandering lives in close contact with nature; to encourage them to embrace the idea of the *home*, as opposed to house. In calling on Aboriginal people to cultivate 'beautiful happy places', Buttsworth was not simply interested in fostering an aesthetic sensibility amongst them. He wished to persuade them to separate the private space of the nuclear family, in which they could feel pride and which was symbolic of their state of moral well being, from the wider public space over which they had no great responsibility or control.

During the 1950s the Board, through *Dawn*, preached a brand of self-help philosophy which was reminiscent of mid-nineteenth-century Britain. The more sympathetic welfarist discourses under which disadvantaged people were seen as victims of broad social and economic processes, rather than as primarily culpable for their situation, did not permeate Aboriginal affairs until the 1960s. Buttsworth clearly saw the Board as having no mission to institute measures of social justice and security such as were being delivered to white people by successive post-war governments. He saw the makeshift dwellings in which many Aboriginal people lived only as:

eyesores on the fringe of country towns. Local people complain unceasingly about these places and will not allow their children to visit the dark children who live there.

The December 1955 issue of *Dawn* is typical of the cultural high handedness of the era. The cover ('Merry Christmas 1955' Figure 3) depicts a young child, amidst balloons, wrapped in cold-weather clothes holding wrapped gifts, a Christmas tree, snowflakes and a twinkling star. Inside readers are given 'Home Hints', such as how to polish linoleum, how to care for indoor plants and how to prevent ants from entering buildings. These were directed at encouraging wives and mothers to cultivate domestic respectability, to keep the interiors of their homes clean and tidy like good suburban housewives. There is an article written by Aboriginal opera singer Harold Blair extolling the virtues of modern life. He wrote:

> The Housing Commission of Victoria found that over 90% of the families from slums made good in new homes and clean surroundings. I believe the same would be true of Aboriginal families. They should be given a chance to have proper houses with electric light and water and all the other things our world can supply.

Another story is headed 'Aboriginal Mother's Dream Comes True' and describes how Alma Ridgeway, a single mother of three sons, moved from the north coast to live in a house in Rozelle in Sydney. She had been able to purchase this 'with the Board's help' (a concession loan scheme was available to those who could save a deposit):

> Mrs. Ridgeway, a shy attractive woman, said she had come to Sydney to 'given my family a chance'. Burnt Bridge aboriginal station has only about 200 people and there is very little work for the young people ... 'We miss the quietness of the bush' she said 'The air here has a tight feeling ... and the soot and noise from the power-house nearby is going to take some getting used to'. [She] had been only a few days in her house when we called, but already it showed signs of her industry. Garden beds had been dug and planted with vegetables and flowers, and the house was as neat as a pin.

This was a rare example of Indigenous home ownership that the Board was keen to publicise. Although low-interest loans were available to prospective Aboriginal home-buyers only 52 had taken them out by 1965 (Joint Committee 1967, p. 11).

Dawn was filled with scenes of conviviality, of music concerts and award presentations; with stories of good workers and housekeepers; with images of appreciation of the Board's work, including photographs of nuclear families standing outside the new houses which had been built for them on the reserve. Those Aboriginal people who recall the sorts of scenes that are depicted in the pages of *Dawn* are today generally scornful of those images and narratives.[8] Most observe that there were very few people who fully believed the assimilationist tales they were being told – that abundant fulfilling suburban lives were in store for those who showed themselves as worthy – even if some learned to be ashamed of their Aboriginality. In order to avoid retribution, many offered token compliance with the expectations of Board officials and even though they took part in the social events that were the focus of *Dawn* articles, they did so with a degree of ironic distance. Even those who sought Exemption Certificates were generally keenly aware of the futility of many of the Board's activities. In the light of this, the propaganda of *Dawn* seems ridiculously naive and based on a misplaced faith in the power of print over Aboriginal people, many of whom were illiterate. Perhaps this faith was typical of the times: an earnest modernist conviction that experts could shape the social lives of subaltern people. However, *Dawn* also conveyed the idea to the broader community: that all was well in Aboriginal affairs, that the Board was exercising benign paternalistic guidance ensuring a bright future for the first inhabitants.

The social engineering practices of the Board were based on the assumption that Aboriginal people would adopt the way of life which was being offered to them and move smoothly into the broader community. This did not happen for two reasons. Firstly, and primarily, the resistance of non-Indigenous people to having Aboriginal neighbours meant that the assimilationist path was not as smooth as had been promised. The next section will show that Aboriginal people confronted a good deal of truculent racist opposition, especially in rural areas, notwithstanding their best efforts to conform. The only way for them to escape this racism was to move in with relatives in the city or, if they were able, to lose themselves and their Aboriginality in suburban areas away from their home towns. So, while the AWB assured them that if they conformed culturally they would be accepted, it was not able to deliver on this promise. Secondly, it was unclear to many that the material benefits of suburban life compensated for the communal ties and perhaps closer connection to traditional land they would continue to enjoy if they remained on the reserve (or on fringe camps in rural areas). Such ties were much harder to sustain elsewhere. Those who left were expected to undergo an enormous cultural transition: from lives of poverty, collective support and camaraderie, to isolated suburban existences. Some successfully underwent this transition. Others found it impossible.

The Aboriginal Housing Crisis in Rural New South Wales

Dawn magazine promoted the idea that the AWB was guiding Aboriginal people towards suburban conformity–conventional family relations, steady employment and domestic order. At a time when social conservatism dominated public life this image appealed to policy makers. But during the sixties political activists and media reports told another story; one of poverty and alienation, and of a people beset by endemic and brooding racist tensions. This was a story that gradually came to shape metropolitan public perceptions. This section will chart the emergence of a rural housing crisis over the 20 years after World War Two. This was a period of state neglect of Aboriginal affairs.

During the early part of the twentieth century, the APB had adopted crude and brutal dispersal policies. After defending the integrity of reserves up until 1910, the Board then shifted direction (Read 1988). Large areas of reserve lands were converted to agriculture, particularly to meet the demand for returned soldier settlers for land after World War One. The Protection Board also ceded some particularly fertile areas of reserves which Aboriginal people were farming successfully for themselves (Goodall 1996, Chapter 10–12). While some reserves were diminished in size, other mostly smaller reserves were closed down completely. This often occurred in response to the growth of the boundaries of country towns in the direction of Aboriginal communities. The Board sought to exile many erstwhile inhabitants, usually those deemed by the colour of their skin to be of lesser Indigenous blood. This was the period too in which the removal of children from their parents became more systematic and widespread and in which the Board diverted many of its resources away from the maintenance and improvement of remaining reserves, and the buildings thereon, and towards 'welfare' activities.

After World War Two, in the 'baby boom' years, there was a growth in the rural Aboriginal population comparable to that in the general community, despite the fact that large numbers of Aboriginal people moved to cities and large towns beneath the gaze of the AWB. While this period saw unprecedented levels of state investment in mainstream housing, particularly in suburban areas, there was no comparable investment in Aboriginal housing. As fertility rates increased, so enormous strains were placed on the land and accommodation resources available to Aboriginal people, both on reserves and elsewhere. At this time, the AWB was responsible for housing on reserves but did not receive enough funding to provide sufficient stock. Many Aboriginal people lived in makeshift shacks or *humpies* of their own construction – made of hessian bags, kerosene tins, corrugated iron and whatever timber could be cobbled together, often from town rubbish dumps – either on reserves or unalienated Crown land. In 1958, Elkin identified thirty-two unofficial camps throughout New South Wales. Those living in these places were not only vulnerable to having their dwellings demolished by local councils, they also endured surveillance and harassment from the AWB through its network of District Welfare Officers. Even those who left or were driven from reserves could not escape the Board's clutches (Goodall 1995). The effects of dispersal policies were appallingly visible to those who travelled through regional and rural parts of the state.

Occasionally, details of the problem surfaced in the metropolitan press. *Truth* newspaper reported on 5 June 1955, for example, that 200 people were living on the reserve at Wellington near Dubbo:

> [I]n conditions of almost indescribable squalor ... Their ancient corrugated iron huts are unfit for pigs, they lack even the most elementary conveniences, and their water supply – drawn by hand from the silt laden Macquarie River – has caused outbreaks of illnesses among the settlement's 100 odd children.

Many camps, some of which were subsequently turned into reserves, were adjacent to rivers situated on flood plains. Higher land was taken to house white townsfolk. The residents of the reserve at Condoblin were situated on a riverbank in houses without bathrooms or laundries. The soil was fine river-silt prone to become very dusty in dry weather and muddy during rains. Those who lived in the Murie, the town's unofficial camp, had to rely for their water on a creek polluted with the town's toilet drainage. At Wilcannia, the inhabitants of the reserve had to suffer floods whenever the adjacent Darling River swelled with rains, including for almost eight months in 1955. In June 1959, *Dawn* magazine (in a rare instance of candid reporting) described an area of swampy land adjacent to the north coast town of Yamba on which a handful of Aboriginal people lived. It had become uninhabitable as a result of rains that had fallen in the area in the previous six months.

Reserve housing was much worse than that enjoyed by mainstream Housing Commission tenants in the suburbs. The Board was allocated £600,000 for housing construction in the four years from 1948–1952, but it took a further 11 years before the same amount was expended again (Joint Committee 1967, pp. 4–5). This was in spite of the fact that the scale of the problem was well known to policy makers. The Commonwealth Ministry of Territories publication, *Our Aborigines*, noted that a survey conducted in New South Wales the previous year had found that over £800,000 would be required to repair or replace unsatisfactory dwellings on reserves and stations (Ministry for Territories 1957). Things did not improve. In 1961, a survey of 739 reserve dwellings found only one in three had bathrooms, more than 80 per cent did not have electricity and that average population density was eight per house. A further survey in 1964 found that much of the stock on the larger reserves, like those at Moree, Bogabilla and Taree, was made of asbestos sheeting and boards without proper kitchens and bathrooms (Joint Committee 1967, pp. 3–10). Three hundred Aborigines Welfare Board-constructed houses did not have kitchen sinks. The absence of internal hot water (or in many cases any water at all) exacerbated health problems.

The lack of accommodation on reserves meant that the Board continued to pursue the practice of dispersal even in the late fifties and early sixties. It sought to restrict numbers by evicting those deemed 'half caste' or of lesser Aboriginal blood under the pretext of encouraging assimilation (Goodall 1995). This meant a growth in the population of unofficial camps, particularly in the west of the state. The 1964 AWB survey found that 38 per cent of Indigenous rural dwellers lived on reserves (Joint Committee 1967, p. 4) as compared with an estimate provided in 1944 that half of Aboriginal people in country New South Wales lived on reserves with the remainder in camps.[9] As fertility rates increased in the late 1940s and, '50s, there were growing numbers with nowhere to go but the camps.

In the mid 1960s, the AWB began to retreat from its conveyor-belt dispersal policy in response to adverse publicity. This followed a case in which a family had been evicted from a reserve on the pretext they were ready to be assimilated into the wider community.[10] With no options for town housing the family went to live in a cave and, as a result of associated health problems, one of the children died. The case was picked up by the metropolitan press and brought considerable public criticism of the Board (Joint Committee 1967, p. 11). In its final annual report (30 June 1968) the AWB conceded 'there are some 1550 adversely accommodated families throughout NSW' (Legislative Committee 1981, p. 34). However, an independent study in the same year found that 18,000 Aboriginal people in the state needed rehousing, the majority in the bush (MacKay 1968).

Good Fences Make Good Neighbours – Keeping Aboriginal People on the Fringes

If Aboriginal people were to take up a place in mainstream society it was necessary for the state to oversee their integration into the residential spaces of country towns, to challenge truculent racism and the established rural social order. The AWB was neither inclined towards, nor equipped for, this task. In the context of this brooding and longstanding atmosphere of conflict, proposals to establish Aboriginal housing within municipal boundaries in the fifties and sixties were generally met with a standard response. Organised residents' resistance led to adverse publicity in local newspapers and local politicians would generally support the townsfolk.

Real-estate agents generally prevented Aboriginal people from obtaining private tenancies and until the late 1960s; few Aboriginal people were offered Housing Commission homes. This was largely because the application and assessment processes were both daunting and discriminatory. Most Aboriginal people were reluctant to expose themselves to the kind of scrutiny which applying for Commission housing involved. Those who did apply were generally deemed unsuitable on cultural grounds. By 1966 only 150 families had been successful in obtaining accommodation from the mainstream housing stock (Joint Committee 1967, p. 31).

A series of confrontations in the fifties and sixties generally failed to break down the marginalisation of Aboriginal people in rural areas. In 1950, for example, the AWB proposed building some new dwellings in Wilcannia to house some of the Paakintji people. This provoked a fierce outcry from the local white community (Rowley 1971, Chapter 12). The

Paakintji were fearful of the consequences of this backlash and at a meeting held by the Board, they recommended that the houses should be built on the existing reserve, even though it was subject to periodic floods (Goodall 1996, p. 281). In situations such as this it was common for Aboriginal people to shun confrontation and to fail to pursue their right to be properly housed within town boundaries.[11]

This sort of local resistance was common. In 1962–1963 the AWB administered only 58 houses within town boundaries throughout New South Wales (Legislative Committee 1981, p. 34). In some places where they were successful in buying land in town, the Board would face a boycott from local building tradespeople forcing it to withdraw development proposals (Goodall 1995, p. 94). Although some headway was made in the next few years, organised community opposition continued to frustrate proposals to build or purchase dwellings until 1969 when the Housing Commission took over the administration of Aboriginal housing. In Bega, on the far south coast of the state, for example, the Board proposed to acquire land in an elite area called the Glebe. This sparked the local mayor into a lather of racist indignation:

> Perhaps this experiment may have best been launched in an area less elite than the one selected where, by gradual process, the hereditary characteristics, instinct, established habits and behaviour common to their race may be thrown off by these people and in due course they may learn to adopt standards more acceptable to the white community (*Bega Advocate* 26 April 1967, p. 1).

This demonstrates that the hostility which Aboriginal people had to deal with was based not simply on racism, but also on class prejudices, a matter that had been alluded to by Elkin in his letter to Coombs discussed above.

In 1968[12] a plan to build AWB houses in South Kempsey led to charges that the Board was failing to meet its obligation to sprinkle only 'respectable' Aboriginal families through the community. A petition was drawn up and a delegation went to state parliament where local parliamentarian JH Brown spoke on the petitioners' behalf. The cause of the white residents was strengthened when Aboriginal people living in Housing Commission homes – having successfully applied for them as conventional applicants – spoke out against the development:

> Mrs R. Archibald who lives in a Housing Commission cottage in nearby Middleton Street was anxious to express her opinions. She and her husband and family moved from Burnt Bridge [Aboriginal community] to Kempsey about a year ago. She is one of the best known leaders of her race in the Kempsey area. She said, 'we don't want to become the centre of an Aboriginal community. We came off the station to make our own way in life and we want to live in a white community with white neighbours' (*McLeay Argus* 15 February 1968, p. 1).

In order for Indigenous people to be accepted in suburban settings they often had to disavow the communal ties which they had grown up with, to choose between communities. A cultural compromise was difficult to find.

The denial of town housing to Aboriginal people was consistent with their marginalisation and persecution in other spheres of life (Goodall 1996, Chapters 11 and 12). Even though they had a right to at least primary-level education, Aboriginal children were excluded from local schools (Fletcher 1989). Police exercised curfews evicting Aboriginal people from the streets of town after dark, even though they had no legal authority to do so. Arrest and imprisonment on spurious charges were a part of everyday life. Non-Indigenous people, by contrast, who were engaged in violence or other racist harassment towards Aboriginal people, generally avoided arrest. Most proposals for Aboriginal housing to be situated within towns came to nothing until 1969, when the state government, in establishing a special Aboriginal housing programme under the control of the Housing Commission, showed a little more preparedness to stare down small-town racism than previously.

'Aboriginal Advancement', Assimilation and Public Education

We have seen how New South Wales failed to promote a measure of social integration until the late sixties. For much of this period the Commonwealth provided the more progressive shape in Aboriginal affairs. However, it was not until 1967 that the Commonwealth Government had significant power to influence the destinies of Indigenous people in New South Wales. Hasluck, considered a progressive on the conservative side of politics, brought a certain idealism to his stewardship of Aboriginal Affairs at a federal level, something lacking in his state counterparts. As a young man, he had spent time travelling throughout Western Australia researching the circumstances and attitudes of Indigenous people. He had come to the conclusion that the old policies of protection and segregation were inappropriate for the mid-twentieth century. He was a champion of the cause of 'Aboriginal advancement' and believed that a separate Indigenous community had for the vast majority 'a dwindling meaning and authority ... while the Australian social organisation had a steadily increasing meaning and authority' (Hasluck 1988, p. 24). 'Fringe dwellers' were, in Hasluck's view, living a life that was neither 'Aboriginal nor Australian'. Every effort, he argued, should be made to remove them from this state of limbo.

Hasluck advocated a gradualist form of assimilation based on recognising that what could be achieved varied according to local circumstance. He saw those located in the south east of the continent, whose people had long lived alongside white communities and had made their living there, as having the right to be received as full Australian citizens. For those in areas where colonial contact was much more recent, Hasluck believed assimilation should proceed at a slower pace although he saw the trend as nevertheless inexorable: Indigenous people would eventually leave behind their culture and community and recognise a broader allegiance. Hasluck believed all governments, state and federal, had a responsibility to foster assimilation but that state Aboriginal welfare legislation only impeded this process. If Aboriginal people were to be harmoniously incorporated into the social mainstream, concessions would have to be made by both Indigenous and non-Indigenous Australians. The former would be obliged to respect the 'Australian way of life', to affirm their principal loyalty to the nation rather than to any separate Aboriginal collectivity, however defined. Hasluck despised the idea of 'a nation within a nation'. The latter would be required to banish the negative stereotypes that informed much knee-jerk racism, to bring an open-minded attitude to the presence of Aboriginal people in their communities.

Hasluck claimed that during the fifties he was prevented from achieving his progressive goals by the intransigence of state administrations and federal government bureaucracies. He recalled that his department officers consistently argued that the Commonwealth 'had to resist any attempt by State governments to use Aborigines as a claim for more financial aid from the Commonwealth' (Hasluck 1988, p. 81). He claimed to be powerless in the face of the parsimonious economics of Treasury and a set of government priorities in which Aboriginal affairs was accorded a low place (p. 84). As a consequence, the circumstances of Indigenous people in the states improved little in this period. Only in the Northern Territory, where the Commonwealth had jurisdiction, was Hasluck able to implement some of his ideas on assimilation.

Some progress was achieved in 1963 in Darwin when a conference of ministers with responsibility for Aboriginal affairs, while agreeing not to pursue uniform national laws, recast the policy of assimilation:

> All Aborigines and part-Aborigines will attain the same manner of living as other Australians and live as members of a single Australian community enjoying the same rights and privileges, accepting the same responsibilities, observing the same customs and influenced by the same beliefs, hopes and loyalties as other Australians. Any special measures taken for Aborigines and part-Aborigines are regarded as temporary measures, not based on race, but intended to meet their need for special care and assistance to protect them from any ill effects of sudden change and to assist them to make the transition from one stage to another in such a way as will be favourable to their social, economic and political advancement (cited in Hasluck 1988, p. 93).

This signalled a belief that the process of assimilation was irreversible, that it might take longer in some places than others but there was little doubt that the modern world would eventually engulf everyone. At this time few questioned the grand narrative of progress or the implications of cultural homogeneity that the narrative implied. Those undergoing assimilation assumed both rights and obligations.[13] In order to be part of this 'single community', Aboriginal people had to accept traditional culture, values and communities as only residual and secondary influences and to acquiesce to the broader obligations of citizenship. In spite of the commitment, there continued to be a wide divergence between state governments on the question of how assimilation was pursued. As in the past, some stressed rights, others obligations.

Although Hasluck had only limited power to influence the fate of most Aboriginal Australians, he, nevertheless, sought to promote greater tolerance among non-Indigenous people. He recognised that popular racist fears were an impediment to assimilation and directed his department to publish and disseminate pamphlets designed to allay such fears. With titles like *Our Aborigines*, *Aboriginal Advancement*, *Australia's Aborigines* and *Fringe Dwellers*, these pamphlets were designed to encourage a civic open-mindedness towards prospective Aboriginal residents of towns and cities, to promote neighbourly coexistence between black and white. The language of the early publications reflected the sense of cultural imperiousness that was characteristic of an earlier era, describing the transition from primitivism to modernity:

> The larger society must be prepared temporarily to adjust its requirements at various points to protect and assist the individual aborigine reaching towards social and economic equality with more advanced Australians (*Our Aborigines*, Department of Territories 1957, p. 10).

By the mid 1960s, a slightly more pluralistic tone was evident:

> Whilst it is, of course, desirable that Aborigines should retain the best of their own culture, it is important for them to realise that tribal obligations have to be considerably modified to meet the basic requirements of a new way of life (*Fringe Dwellers*, Department of Territories 1964, p. 15).

The central obstacles to the process of assimilation and the source of most conflict with other Australians, centred on where and how Aboriginal people should be housed, and their children educated. The government publications dealt with these issues. The authors of *Australia's Aborigines* (Department of Territories 1965) argued that Aboriginal people had been guilty of neglecting and destroying public housing. This reinforced the stereotypes and fears which non-Indigenous people held:

> Aborigines have, at first, so befouled them that they have quickly made them untenable; that many will, quite casually, tear off doors and literally tear down the houses themselves to burn if they are short of firewood; that, until they are well advanced, they will generally abandon a house completely if a death has occurred in it (p. 32).

However, the writers of the pamphlet sought to convince readers that these tendencies were only present amongst those living in remote areas, people who inevitably encountered social and economic difficulties in transferring from a 'primitive wurlie into a modern house'. The obstacles to assimilation were not so acute for those 'more advanced or completely detribalised Aborigines in the closely settled areas'. But even here:

> Special housing schemes are necessary ... and vigorous help from all other Australians, to enable the Aborigines to emerge from their shanties to non-segregated homes and positions of social, economic, and healthy independence (p. 33).

This literature described a vision of active community involvement in the process of assimilation. It was one that went beyond mere neighbourliness to entail a level of cultural surveillance, which was likely to provoke resentment:

> Much more than the right attitude and expressions of sympathy are needed. Concrete practical assistance for the material welfare of the fringe dwellers, personal and individual aid to these people to help them cross the threshold to assimilation, constant vigilance to prevent them sliding back to the old way of life, belief in their right to be part of the community, and enthusiasm in the protection and promotion of that right, are all essential to the solution to the problem (*Fringe Dwellers*, Department of Territories 1964, p. 32).

Hasluck and Commonwealth bureaucrats saw Aboriginal people as having the obligation to develop regular habits as a price of their acceptance into the social mainstream:

> Fringe dwellers need to be encouraged to establish themselves permanently in one place, to adopt a moderate and reasonable viewpoint on their obligations to visit relatives, and to see these obligations in the proper perspective relative to other obligations such as that of giving their children reasonable continuity in education. This 'walkabout' urge can be eliminated only by giving these people permanent and secure places in the community (*Fringe Dwellers* p. 21).

The grass-roots 'helping hand' approach advocated by the government pamphlets was consistent with a liberal politics characteristic of the sixties. Those whitefellas who felt sympathy for Indigenous rights also felt themselves to be free to express and act on those feelings. Later, when the more radical politics of self-determination emerged in the seventies, non-Indigenous people were excluded from the political vanguard. Activism influenced by sixties liberal values could move non-Indigenous people to collaborate in national movements such as the campaign to institute the 1967 national referendum to give the Commonwealth more control over Aboriginal affairs.

It could also move them to organise local 'support' groups. Such groups were found in parts of the country where non-Indigenous people took a stand against the dominant racism. They were generally made up of middle-class people who were well-meaning but patronising and paternalistic. In Armidale northern New South Wales, for example, a group of wives of academics at the University of New England formed the Armidale Association for the Assimilation of Aborigines. They agitated for improved housing for those who wished to move away from a fringe camp located adjacent to the local municipal rubbish dump (Franklin 1995). In Narrogin in Western Australia a local citizens' council was established to work with the state housing authority to smooth the transition of a group of Aboriginal people into dwellings constructed within town boundaries (Bell 1989). Mostly, as in Narrogin, these social experiments ended in failure, with white citizens, whose 'assistance' was ill-informed and ham-fisted, exasperated at the failure of the Indigenous people to take up the opportunities made available to them.

In spite of the efforts of Hasluck, the Department of Territories and members of Aboriginal 'progress' groups to encourage greater tolerance and, therefore, to clear the pathway to assimilation, the popular desire for racist segregation persisted until well after the New South Wales government decided it was time for a change. The public affirmation in 1969 that Indigenous people had the right to town housing did not ensure that they were able easily to exercise that right. As Chapter 4 will demonstrate, racist exclusion on cultural grounds continued in a more subtle way even after the provision and management of Aboriginal housing were taken away from the AWB and passed over to the mainstream bureaucracy. Officials of the Housing Commission (and non-Indigenous tenants), far from operating as even-handed, tolerant and rational bureaucrats, generally expected Indigenous people to adapt instantly to the norms of suburban life. There was little acknowledgment that the Commission's rules and forms of evaluation were ethnocentric and likely to exclude and alienate Aboriginal applicants and tenants.

Joint Parliamentary Committee

By the mid 1960s, the state could no longer sustain the colonialist fantasy that Aboriginal people could or would assimilate smoothly. The contradictions inherent in running Indigenous affairs as a separate field of public administration came to a head in New South Wales at this time. In 1965 a group of students led by future Aboriginal leader Charles Perkins, travelled though country New South Wales in what is now known as the Freedom Rides (Curthoys 2002). Modelled on civil rights protests in the United States, the protest action aimed to draw the attention of the metropolitan public to segregation and discrimination in small towns. In addition, the protesters visited reserves and stations to highlight the appalling living conditions of the inhabitants. These events took place in an era of growing liberalism in public opinion and a waning of Cold War conservatism. During the 15 years after World War Two, state governments had viewed Aboriginal people as not party to the general social contracts which they struck with their citizens. Their living conditions were not measured by the same benchmarks as were applied to others. They were widely viewed as inhabiting a separate sphere. During the 1960s, however, the tenor of public debate began to change. Aboriginal affairs were subject to a more universalist-liberal political discourse that challenged the double standards and apartheid of the past. While in the Protection years Indigenous people were generally deemed to be outside the national imagined community, Assimilation had raised the inference that 'fringe dwellers' had at least the potential for citizenship and the right to a better life. The social circumstances that the Freedom Riders exposed almost certainly shocked many city dwellers and generated widespread sympathy for Aboriginal people.

In 1965, a Joint Committee of the New South Wales Legislative Assembly and Council was formed 'to inquire into and report on the welfare of Aborigines in the state'. This was a broad brief. The way in which Aboriginal people were housed was a central concern of the committee and formed a key theme of submissions from and discussion with many of the witnesses who appeared before it. One of these was JT Purcell, the chair of the Housing Commission. His organisation had long resisted the suggestion that it provide any special consideration for Aboriginal applicants and in evidence given to the committee Purcell argued that the majority of those who lived in reserve housing or in unofficial camps were unsuited for town housing. He believed that to undertake such a transition they would need instruction and regulation and that many did not want to leave their makeshift dwellings:

> You cannot think of better housing or improved housing without the necessary education that must go with it to teach the appreciation of its value and necessary responsibilities (Joint Committee 1967, Part II, p. 28).

He clearly saw his administrative role as involving responsibilities that went beyond mere provision of housing. The Housing Commission was also involved in the business of moral regulation:

> It would be out of keeping with the proper intention and purpose of public housing to allow occupation of town houses by aborigines, any more than by white people, who would not be likely to accept rental responsibilities, conform to normal requirements of occupation or ordinary and proper standards of hygiene, civic pride and social behaviour (p. 29).

Purcell recommended that Aboriginal tenants be given transitional dwellings and taught to prepare for mainstream housing. This was, in effect, little different from the situation that had prevailed in the past. The AWB had always provided sub-standard accommodation on reserves.

In support of this he described a trip to Wilcannia two months earlier when he visited the Mallee, an unofficial settlement of makeshift dwellings to the west of the town. In his verbal evidence to the Joint Committee he described his encounter here with a group of Paakantji people who were seated beneath a tree playing records. Most were young but Purcell spoke to the eldest, an old woman and asked her whether she would be interested in accepting 'transitional housing', intermediate dwellings constructed as part of a programme of phased assimilation:

> These people are very loath to leave. They say they do not want to move from these humpies and shanties ... I asked the old lady whether she would take one of these houses ... She said that she did not want to move and would not take a house – that it was too hot ... Nothing that I could say to the lady could convince her there was a better way of life if she took a cottage in the town or on some local reserve or locality (Joint Committee 1967, p. 31).

Purcell's words demonstrate a misunderstanding of the situation of the Aboriginal people of Wilcannia and of the politics of exclusion. The reluctance of many Aboriginal people in small towns like Wilcannia (particularly in remote areas) to embrace the idea of town housing, evidence of which Purcell came across in late 1965, must be understood against the backdrop of longstanding local tensions. They would rather remain in poverty amongst their own people than be exposed to the hostility of white neighbours, the effects of which had been apparent to them time and again. In addition in towns like Wilcannia, where racism was endemic, Aboriginal people would often tell public officials (like Purcell) what they wanted to hear.

In spite of the resistance of the Housing Commission, the Joint Committee recommended in its 1967 report that future dwellings should be of Commission standard. It also recommended that no more dwellings be built on reserves and that the functions of social and child welfare should be separated from the administration of housing. The committee accepted, however, another submission made by Purcell, that new house purchasing and construction work should be concentrated in cities and in larger country towns, and that Aboriginal people should be encouraged to move away from small, remote communities to places with better job prospects.

In the same year as the Joint Committee's report was published, more than 90 per cent of Australian people voted by referendum to amend the constitution so as to transfer from the states to the federal government the power to legislate in the area of Aboriginal affairs. Although the Liberal/Country Party administration of the late sixties did not fully exercise this power, and some oppressive state legislation remained in place until the election of the Whitlam Labor government in 1972, there was a significant move against the exclusionist policies of the past (Attwood and Marcus 1997). Aboriginal people could now lay a formal claim to full citizenship rights.

Conclusion

Chapter 1 discussed the moral alarm that was provoked by fringe dwelling and suggested that the eradication of reminders of Aboriginal presence was central to the process of turning colonial settlements into towns and cities. The original development of the reserve system, ostensibly to 'protect' and to reconstitute traditional social ecology, was consistent with this goal. When it became clear that the Aboriginal race would not die out of its own accord the state pursued child removal and dispersal policies to hasten the breakdown of the Indigenous social order. In the late thirties, after assimilation was formally adopted as policy, reserves became places of confinement and cultural indoctrination something that was consistent with dominant modernist thinking of the era. Those promoting modernism sought cultural convergence and the abnegation of difference.

However, Aboriginal people remained beleaguered and excluded in spite of the formal commitment of the state to oversee their absorption into the social mainstream. The determination of residents of country towns to patrol the symbolic boundary between themselves and the other belied the narrative of advancement that informed the actions of those in Aboriginal affairs. Indigenous people were caught between the public dreams of modernisation and the stubborn obstacles presented by local racism. In promoting (albeit largely rhetorically) the idyll of harmonious neighbourly coexistence between black and white, policy makers also underestimated the reluctance of Aboriginal people to relinquish the cultural forms that were the basis of solidarity and that were incompatible with conventional urban/suburban lives. Although key Commonwealth politicians and bureaucrats supported the migration into towns, the legal, political and administrative structures that existed prior to the late 1960s prevented this. The AWB was ineffectual and failed to stand up to small-town apartheid. Indeed, it reinforced the prevalent cultural prejudices. When Coombs and Hasluck sought to initiate progressive change, the states refused to cede power over Indigenous affairs to the centre. New South Wales governments were unwilling to tackle the racism which was endemic to country towns and which operated with the imprimatur of police and local authorities. The cumbersome machinery of Australian federalism ensured the stagnation of Aboriginal affairs for much of the twentieth century.

In post-war Australia, Indigenous people experienced a double standard. While others enjoyed the benefits of citizenship, including improved welfare entitlements and state sponsored housing, they were denied such things. They were poor, powerless and excluded from the imagined community of nation. By the late sixties, circumstances forced authorities to address such exclusion. Images of deprivation inflamed metropolitan opinion and brought Aboriginal affairs into the reforming sights of post-war liberalism/progressivism. However, as we shall see in later chapters, the reforms of the late 1960s failed to significantly rectify the structures that both excluded and alienated Aboriginal people.

Chapter 3

Profane Presence: Urbanisation and Pan-Aboriginality

After World War Two

The previous chapter showed how dispersal and assimilation policies rendered Aboriginal people in the bush increasingly marginal and powerless. In these circumstances cities appeared to offer something of a refuge, particularly from the 1940s as the growth in demand for urban workers tempted many to flee the misery and poverty of the camps and the confinements and humiliations of the reserves in search of a better life.[1] This was especially true of young people who could not tolerate the discrimination they experienced (Lippman 1973). City life also offered them excitement and relative freedom from racist surveillance. But their presence challenged official ideology. Those who entered cities were officially viewed as being in the process of becoming assimilated. So the clusters of Indigenous housing in places like Redfern, Waterloo and Alexandria were a profane presence that undermined the narrative of smooth transition that was central to Aboriginal affairs. As we saw in Chapter 1, nineteenth-century press reports used the language of pathos to describe 'fringe dwellers' as a dying remnant. Those who chose to live in or around the centres of settlement were either pitied or demonised. By the mid-twentieth century, however, the purveyors of this concern were promoting popular fears about the emergence of black ghettos akin to Harlem in New York – a dark and threatening presence within. At this time authorities, and to a large extent academic urban ethnographers, viewed the growing numbers of Aboriginal people living in cities as tacitly accepting a social contract under which they would become culturally indistinguishable from Anglo-Australians. However, living within the space of colonial society and not adhering to its moral economy has long been a strategic post-colonial response to the history of dispossession. From the 1960s Indigenous urban dwellers began to develop a pan-Aboriginal vernacular culture and radical politics that was distinct from that of both their white neighbours and of their communities of origin.

Migration to Sydney

The precise pattern and rate of the movement of Aboriginal people to Sydney is difficult to ascertain. This is mainly because until 1971 Aboriginal people were not included in the census data that was collected every five years, although some limited statistics were gathered in 1961 and '66. Until its repeal in the 1967 referendum, section 127 of the Commonwealth Constitution stated that '... in recording the number of people of the Commonwealth, or of a State or other part of the Commonwealth, Aboriginal natives shall not be counted'.[2] The AWB periodically collected demographic statistics about those living on reserves but not about those living in unofficial camps or in cities and towns.

There were probably small numbers of Aboriginal people living as tenants in houses in the poorer districts of Sydney in the early twentieth century, in addition to those who camped at Circular Quay and elsewhere in the vicinity of the city at this time. There is some photographic evidence suggesting that there were Aboriginal people resident in the Sydney's Rocks district around 1900 when much of the area was razed by the state government in response to an outbreak of bubonic plague. Taksa's research into the history of the Everleigh Street Railway Workshops in Redfern indicated that there were a number of Indigenous employees working there and living nearby at this time (Taksa 1996). Government dispersal policies in the 1920s drove more into the inner city. Although there were small Indigenous communities living in rented housing in working-class suburbs like Balmain, Redfern and Waterloo in the 1920s and '30s, the major wave of migration began from the 1940s. Plater quotes Daniel Syron as recalling:

> When I was young I don't remember a lot of Aborigines in Redfern in say, the late 30s ... There was certainly no Everleigh Street community [which in recent times has housed a large Indigenous population] in those days (Plater 1995, p. 42).

During World War Two and in the immediate post-war decades many Aboriginal people moved from the bush to live in urban areas where jobs were more plentiful and wages were much higher than in the country. This was true of Sydney as well as other state capitals (Gale 1964, pp. 122–123). In addition some were involved in urban civil reconstruction work after 1945. A newspaper reported in 1948 that a family of four that earned an income of eight pounds a week in the bush could increase this to 21 pounds a week in the city:

> An aboriginal girl received 30/- a week as a cook on a station. She moved to a country town and got 35/- per week as washer up in a cafe. Coming to Sydney she got four pounds ten shillings a week in a shirt factory (*Smith's Weekly*, 22 May 1948).

The city provided Aboriginal people, particularly young people, with the opportunity to escape the stifling racism of small towns and move to places where they were not watched so intensively by police and welfare authorities.

The metropolitan population grew through a process of chain migration. Once families were established in housing they would host relatives, who either visited for short periods, perhaps to obtain medical attention or to buy clothes and other goods from second-hand shops. Others settled permanently. There were many couples with young families who sought improved educational opportunities for their children. Half of the Aboriginal people in Sydney were under the age of 15 years as compared with 30 per cent for the Australian population as a whole (Beasley 1970, p. 148).[3] Seventy-one per cent were under 30. These family groupings tended to be matrifocal (Eckermann 1977). In circumstances of poverty it was women who would marshal resources to make sure everyone was fed.[4]

The movement of Indigenous population to metropolitan centres occurred across Australia. Aboriginal communities were established in places like Fitzroy and Footscray in Melbourne, Fortitude Valley in Brisbane, Adelaide's West End and in Allawah Grove and to the east of Perth, a city where a night-time curfew operated to exclude Aboriginal people from the CBD after 6 pm. In Sydney, many settled in the older inner suburbs, areas like Redfern, Waterloo, Surry Hills, Erskineville and Newtown, places with much decaying nineteenth-century housing, large terraces which had been neglected by their slum landlords. Although the inner-city Aboriginal population came to be made up of people from a number of regions, the majority of those who came from the south coast settled in La Perouse (Beasley 1970, pp. 140–146). Redfern and surrounding suburbs housed many Budjalung and others from the north coast of New South Wales as well as those who came from the west of the state, particularly from Wiradjuri lands. Most arrived in Sydney at nearby Central Station.

It is difficult to pinpoint the size of the Sydney Aboriginal population at any one point in the 1950s and 60s. This is because the high level of transmigration between city and bush meant that there was a high turnover of residents: people moving to and fro as seasonal employment and community and cultural obligations led many city dwellers to return to their home lands regularly and often for extended periods. Rowley wrote that the move to the city 'remains experimental for many, who may come and go until assets in the metropolis, social and economic, will so far outweigh those in the areas of origin that the city becomes the home' (Rowley 1971, p. 364). Various estimates of the size of the Sydney population were made by academics. In 1950, Wait reported that an Aborigines Welfare Board informal census in 1945 revealed there were 2500 Aboriginal residents in the metropolitan area. The author believed that this had grown to 3000 by 1950 (Wait 1950, p. 7). The influx from that point was quite rapid. Robinson claimed that 12,000 Aboriginal people lived just in the Redfern area in 1965 (Robinson 1972) but Wells assessed the entire metropolitan population in the mid sixties at 'between 10,000 and 11,000' (Wells 1966). Pamela Beasley's extensive study of Aboriginal households in Sydney in the late sixties found that there were 'at least 6000 (possibly as many as 10,000) people of Aboriginal descent living in Sydney' (Beasley 1970, p. 138). In 1971 Lovejoy cited an unpublished University of Sydney study which found approximately 12,000 residents in the state's capital (Lovejoy 1971, p. 81).

Whatever the total Aboriginal population in Sydney, it is clear that the numbers grew rapidly in the 25 years after the end of World War Two. For much of that time the state either did not acknowledge the presence of distinct Indigenous communities or viewed them as assimilated by virtue of their location and, therefore, in need of little special social welfare support. For much of this period the AWB had very little effective control over those who lived in metropolitan enclaves (except, of course, for those living at the La Perouse reserve). While in country towns District Welfare Officers played an important surveillance role over those Indigenous people who lived off reserves, their influence over the ballooning population in inner Sydney was limited. Aboriginal leader Chicka Dixon recalls 'I went to the government in 1967 and pointed out that there was a need for hostels for Aborigines because of the mass migration of teenagers from the riverbanks to Sydney' (Tatz 1975, p. 33). The growth in the Aboriginal population at La Perouse reflected the general urbanisation trend. Bell reported in 1961 that the area had undergone a fourfold increase in population between 1930 and 1956 (Bell 1961). The longstanding policy of restricting the numbers on the reserve to established residents had not been effective as the growth of the adjacent unofficial camp at Frog Hollow indicated.

The presence of Aboriginal people in places like Redfern, Waterloo and Newtown was something of a paradox. The state had long defined Aboriginality in spatial terms as much as in terms of blood or culture. Colonial ideology held that any person who identified as Indigenous and who associated with other Indigenous people, belonged not in the streets of towns and cities but outside the urban boundaries. Those who wished to live alongside whites implicitly signalled their preparedness to sever cultural links and to live like respectable middle-class citizens. The presence of a growing inner urban population was disturbing. Popular and official concerns were magnified because Aboriginal people took up residence, not (for obvious reasons) in the respectable neighbourhoods, but in notorious slum areas. This meant that Indigenous city dwellers were doubly marginalised: both on the basis of their race and because they were associated with the 'undeserving poor' who inhabited these regions. Once they had been identified as a distinctive sub-culture they were represented by the popular press (and in some academic accounts) as a deviant and potentially subversive presence. Like their nineteenth-century predecessors who made their homes in the city streets, those Aboriginal people who lived in crowded inner-city housing, were seen by the guardians of respectability as threatening miscegenation and moral degeneration.

'Slums' and 'Ghettos'

In May 1948 *Smith's Weekly*, a widely read sensationalist tabloid newspaper of the post-war era, reported that there had been a big Aboriginal influx from the bush to Sydney since the war ended. This:

> flooded the slum suburb of Redfern with between 500 and 600 natives of all castes and ages, and created a serious social problem there. Whole families are still arriving daily and crowding into the wretched accommodation occupied by aborigines already settled in the slums. One squalid shack with a 10 foot frontage – already housing four families totalling 20 men, women and children – is to accommodate a fifth family next week . . . the natives, ignorant of city life, communal hygiene and the wiles of unscrupulous whites are introducing a new low in slum standard living (22 May 1948, p. 1).

The report went on to state that those who came from 'humpies in the bush' found the city slums quite congenial and that they also found greater acceptance and less discrimination in their new homes.

The new arrivals had settled in places that had long been the focus of respectable concerns. Expressions of alarm about the Aboriginal population and their living conditions were part of a broader slum clearance and town planning discourse which had its roots in the late nineteenth century. In the last 30 years of the nineteenth century Sydney underwent a huge growth in the population as many of those who had arrived in Australia during the mid-century gold rushes moved into urban centres when the rushes ended. Whether as a cause or effect of population growth, the 1870s and '80s saw the first substantial development of manufacturing industry in Sydney and the establishment of an urban proletariat. In 1890 almost half the metropolitan population lived in areas of row houses and tenements of around 40 people per acre (Davison 1995, pp. 60–61).[5] By 1900 it had become one of the largest cities in the British Empire.

The planning of Sydney became an important issue at this time as the housing and municipal infrastructure proved inadequate to cope with the growth. From the 1870s there was widespread concern about the growth of slum housing in the city and adjacent suburbs. The *Bulletin*, an important organ of radical nationalism in the late nineteenth and early twentieth centuries, waged a campaign against Sydney's lack of planning and the overcrowding. In doing so it provided rich descriptions of urban squalor. In 1888 the newspaper described the new areas in the following terms:

> Glued side by side with a brain straining uniformity are streets upon streets of stifling, stuffy, soggy terraces with Lilliputian yards badly drained, rooms badly lighted, ventilated not at all; rows rather of fever-dens and zymotic disease depots than human habitations.[6]

The publication had earlier that year editorialised prophetically on the inappropriateness of high density housing for Australian conditions:

> A great fuss is being made about the erection of dwelling houses on the tenement system for the Sydney working man. In the Australian climate these huge barracks would be hells on earth. What our workman wants, and is entitled to, and will have in the long run, is a detached cottage with a piece of land. Fancy an Australian working man tramping up four flights of stairs on his way to bed! Fancy the atmosphere of such a menagerie, the smells of fifty dinners, some hundred pairs of boots of soiled clothes, of gutter gambling children! Faugh! Tenements for working men? So English you know.[7]

The town planning movement emerged in the early twentieth century as part of the modernist crusade of the respectable middle classes to reshape the living environments of the lower orders. Town planning was based on progressivist belief that if the deserving poor were taken away from the decaying, foetid slums of the inner city and placed in clean, suburban environments they would experience better health and embrace respectable morality and stable nuclear family life. The development of some early garden and broad-acre suburbs took place in the 1910s and '20s but the involvement of the state in large-scale redevelopment of Sydney occurred much later.

The 1930s saw a renewed push for slum clearance as the Great Depression created an impoverished under-class. For the advocates of scientific welfare, like Oswald Barnett, a Melbourne accountant who campaigned for slum clearance through the 1930s and '40s, the future prosperity and stability of the nation depended on the development of new housing for the poor (Barnett 1933; Barnett and Burt 1942). Although, as Spearritt observed, very few of what were widely viewed as Sydney's slums were demolished prior to World War Two, the advocates of slum clearance had managed to establish a 'conventional wisdom about urban housing policy which favoured suburban house and gardens over the terraces of the inner suburbs' (Spearritt 1973, p. 42). One of those advocates, NH Dick, defined the slums of Sydney as lying 'adjacent to one another in what may be called the "inner suburbs". Commencing in Woolloomooloo Bay they spread through Surry Hills, Paddington, Redfern, Newtown, Glebe, Pyrmont, Balmain, Alexandria, Waterloo and Botany' (*Sydney Morning Herald*, July 25 1935).

Many of these places became the homes for groups of Aboriginal people in the post-war era. Planner and architect Walter Bunning, who had been executive officer for the Commonwealth Housing Commission, described the inner regions of Sydney in 1945 as characterised by:

> narrow, ugly streets, lanes, alleys and mean pocket handkerchief allotments. In this whole square mile you will not find one park or playground. The children play in the lanes and alleys; they live a lane life and their parents sit on the doorsteps. Few of these houses have gardens at the front ... At the back they try to grow flowers – they grow sooty stunted flowers like their own withered lives (Bunning 1945, p. 5).

During her visit to Australia in 1954, the newly crowned Queen, an adored figure at the time, travelled into Sydney by rail at one point in her tour. Rather than expose the delicate royal eyes to the slum blight of Redfern's Aboriginal districts on the approaches to Central Station, local authorities erected great hessian screens to obscure her view. It was not until the gentrification of the 1970s that the older dwellings of the inner city came to be revalued.

Public concerns about, and policing of, urban sub-cultural communities had a long history. In nineteenth century Europe the ruling classes held longstanding fears about the social disorders which they believed were concealed in the labyrinthine quarters of the poor, particular in those situations where the intense sociability of working-class life was unsurveilled and unregulated. In England the expansion of cities in the north east and Midlands in the early and mid 1800s had produced an alarming growth of slums and appalling, very visible poverty (Engels 1958). The rebuilding of Paris after the revolution of 1848 by Georges-Eugene (Baron) Hausmann was largely an exercise in social control. The wide boulevards of the Paris of today were originally constructed in order to cut slices through residential districts which harboured revolutionary culture during the Second Empire of Napoleon III, and to force the poor out of the city's centre. Modernist town planning was, from its origins in mid-nineteenth century Europe, organised to alleviate the fears of respectable citizens about the disorder in their midst.

Likewise in late nineteenth-century Sydney those who called upon the city council for slum clearance were more concerned with social control than with social welfare. Public debate about the urban problems was frequently characterised by the language of contagion. The colonial gentry feared that respectable young people would succumb to the immoral habits of the 'undeserving poor' if there was too much mixing in public space. Organic metaphors were frequently used to describe the city itself. The slum districts would spread cancer-like to more respectable districts. The social and physical diseases that were concocting in the dark, damp and airless courtyards of the poor would threaten the health and morals of all the citizens. Descriptions of Sydney around the turn of the century were often filled with miasmic images.

Twentieth-century campaigns for the improvement of urban environments can be seen, therefore, as having two central motivations. Firstly they emerged out of moral panics about slums and the degradation of domestic life therein. Secondly they represented middle-class concerns about general social disorder in cities. Urban modernism was largely a response to the teeming overcrowded quarters of the poor. For its early advocates it was about establishing a polite, promenading street culture in place of the raucous and irreverent behaviour being exhibited by many of the young people in the cities.

The appearance of Aboriginal people added a racist layer to the existing panics about the lumpenproletariat. The Indigenous presence in Redfern and nearby areas sparked not only an intensification of pre-existing public concerns about theft, drunkenness and crime but also prompted fears about miscegenation. *Smith's Weekly* followed up its 1948 report on urban migration with another in 1950. The edition of 8 April carried a front-page banner headline which read 'Sydney's Harlem: Black Men, White Girls'. At this time the black ghetto areas of New York City conjured up frightening images: public disorder, drugs, unrestrained sexuality. The article shared much with urban anxieties from an earlier era (Mayne 1993). In the late nineteenth century the press were liable to depict the Chinese districts of cities as dangerous places filled with amoral heathens ready to lure unwary and innocent Europeans into gambling houses and opium dens. The imagery was one of contagion: of whites by other racial groups, of respectable districts of cities by those inhabited by the 'debauched' underclasses. The fear of larrikin youth gangs in late nineteenth-century Sydney was based partly on the popular perception that there were areas which were outside the reach of the law and conventional morality (Morgan 1997). *Smith's Weekly* stated that Negro American soldiers had visited Redfern and adjacent suburbs during the war and had been involved with white women in the area:

> That invasion had left its own half caste harvest. Today more that 800 of our own aboriginal men and women have migrated to these suburbs ... White women have deserted their husbands to live with black men and Australian adolescents have cruelly exploited coloured girls who are easily flattered by a white man's attention.

The salacious report went on to give details of white teenage girls getting married to Aboriginal men and of Aboriginal women seeking out white husbands:

> A few weeks ago, a 17-year-old girl in Surry Hills was married to a black man and three weeks later give birth to a child which she cheekily named after the wife of the minister who married her ... Dark girls are easy prey for white larrikins. Some of them, particularly those with a mixture of blood are very attractive and are easily flattered by whites. But the men regard them as chattels.

The concern about the sexual permissiveness within inner-city Aboriginal communities found expression in academic literature such as Ronald and Catherine Berndt's study of South Australia (Berndt 1951). The West End of Adelaide was similar to the Redfern region of Sydney with a relatively high Indigenous population living in overcrowded run-down houses. The Berndts expressed concern about the sexual freedom and miscegenation:

> today a number of 'aborigines' in the city have been steadily approaching a state which can only be described as promiscuous; and this process was accelerated, during the war, by the moral laxity prevalent in some quarters of the white community . . . there is a tendency to regard [aboriginal woman] as actual or potential prostitutes (p. 251).

They went on to condemn white men as hypocrites for visiting black prostitutes but frowning on mixed marriages. They noted the tendency for younger Indigenous people to favour mixed marriages and they saw this as accelerating the process of absorption (*see also* Eckermann 1977).

The expressions of alarm that were focussed on urban Aboriginal people were symptomatic of the prevailing conservatism of post-war Australia. They were also reminiscent of nineteenth-century fears that fringe dwellers would attract wayward young people into vicious habits. Similar concerns have been expressed in recent times about the drug culture associated with The Block area of Redfern. For their part the young people who made their way to Sydney in the 1940s, '50s and '60s experienced a great sense of liberation. Those who remember Redfern at this time talk of the Aboriginal gatherings in pubs like the Empress Hotel in Redfern and the Cricketers Arms in Alexandria (Plater 1995). Eventually many such places incurred the attention of local police – a pattern that has continued to the present day – and some were closed down. However, the restrictions that were placed on young people in the city were much less stringent than those that they experienced in rural areas. Rugby League matches provided an opportunity for communal gatherings with the All Blacks team, based in Redfern and established in the early 1950s. The All Blacks played regular matches against a team from La Perouse and later an annual competition was established involving Aboriginal teams from all over New South Wales. Rowley observed that such activities attracted the criticism of authorities as not being in the interests of assimilation (Rowley 1971, p. 367). Hartley (2002) has argued that these sporting gatherings were central to the emergence of a radical Aboriginal political culture, fostering the development of networks that were central in the struggle against assimilation. The city provided a place not only where young people could find better paid jobs, but also they could find their way in the world free from the constraints which were imposed on them by the authorities (and in some instances their own elders) in their home lands.

Ethnographies of Cultural Loss

In the 25 years after the end of World War Two, the state generally neglected Aboriginal people in urban areas. Although there were growing Indigenous clusters in the inner city, policy makers generally did not recognise them as a distinct social group with particular problems and needs. Hasluck recalled, for example, that 'the part-coloured minority in Melbourne was regarded as one aspect of a social situation and was not seen as a racial situation' (Hasluck 1988, pp. 73–74). A central assumption behind the policy of assimilation was that those who chose to live in the cities and towns thereby signalled a preparedness to cede their Indigenous identities and become absorbed into the social mainstream. The field of Aboriginal affairs dealt predominantly with those who lived on reserves or in rural camps. It was not until the early 1960s that there was a firm recognition of the urban Indigenous presence in public policy.

In spite of this some academic researchers began to focus on those living in cities and towns from the late 1940s. Up to that point, studies of Aboriginal people were largely confined to conventional anthropology. These studies focused on remote area communities and traditional culture. From the late 1940s, however, some ground-breaking work in social anthropology (and later geography–*see* Gale 1964; and sociology–Eckermann 1977) explored the processes of urbanisation and assimilation. Most such work was undertaken by women (Barwick 1962; Berndt 1962; Fink 1955; Reay 1945; Reay and Stiltington 1948) and much of it was conducted in Adelaide (Berndt and Berndt 1951; Gale 1964; Inglis 1961). This was an era when most women were discouraged from undertaking fieldwork in remote areas with more traditional communities. While most of their male colleagues were off conducting hairy-chested feats of ethnography in remote areas, women broke the new ground of urban anthropology.

There was an almost universal perception among researchers that those who had moved into cities had experienced cultural loss. In keeping with the dominant functionalism of the time, these studies depicted new Indigenous urban migrants as being in a state of stalled transition between tradition and modernity, and most accorded with the public norms and policy imperatives of the Assimilation era. Ethnographic writing generally lamented the decline of traditional knowledge and the lack of regard which young Aboriginal people had for their elders. It appeared to the researchers that the loss of attachment to land sounded the death knell of the old ways. Without those ways there was no substance to Indigenous culture.

The effects of consumerism and mass culture, particularly on young Aboriginal people, loomed large in much academic analysis. The Berndts claimed that the majority of the Indigenous population of Adelaide had by the late 1940s, lost contact with their cultural heritage (Berndt and Berndt 1951, Chapter VII). In their book they placed inverted commas around 'aborigines' when referring to those of mixed parentage who lived in the city, and wrote disparagingly of their desire for cheap consumer goods:

> Some of them buy more than they can afford or need, chiefly from the second-hand stores, but also liquor, movies, sensational magazines, soft drinks, ice creams, candy and other 'luxuries' (p. 242).

They noted that many Aboriginal women were good and thrifty managers of household incomes. Others, however, wanted to 'have things the way film stars have got them' and wasted their money on colourful, showy but shoddy things for their houses in the hope that this would distract attention from the more squalid aspects of their surroundings (p. 243). This criticism is reminiscent of that which some social commentators levelled at the English working class in the post-war era. Richard Hoggart, for example, lamented the way youth from the poor districts of industrial cities forsook the simple cooperative pleasures of neighbourhood life for the superficial attractions of (largely American) popular culture (Hoggart 1958).

Like the Berndts he looked back fondly to an era where the lines of cultural transmission between parents and children were intact. Both viewed modern society as having a corrupting impact on traditional cultures and neither had much faith in the ability of the young to develop cultural forms which were worthy of their roots, nor to embrace those forms without trading their collective identities.

Inglis's research conducted ten years after that of the Berndts describes a remarkable degree of affluence amongst the Indigenous population of Adelaide. This was in the middle of the post-war economic boom. Most families in her study had washing machines, television, refrigerators and chrome and laminex kitchens, and all had radios. Her writing contains fewer judgemental comments on the young Indigenous people of Adelaide who 'go to the same "rock and roll" dance hall or fun parlour, or loiter around the railway stations at weekends' (Inglis 1961, p. 203). However, she notes the tendency of Aboriginal households to get deeply 'into hock' to obtain consumer goods and to 'keep up with the Jones's' (p. 208). Work in other locations, by contrast, confirmed that Aboriginal people were considerably poorer than their non-Indigenous working-class neighbours (Beasley 1971).[8]

Like the Berndts, Inglis noted that a substantial minority embraced the assimilationist model and made a break with old ways. They moved to the suburbs and distanced themselves from their relatives while seeking to pass as non-Indigenous. Some women, she argued, sought out white husbands because this invariably led to upward social mobility (Inglis 1961, pp. 204–208). Barwick, too, remarked that some of those living in Melbourne were willing to pass but that most rejected assimilation because 'the implied recognition of inferiority affects their self esteem'. Nevertheless, most of those whom the ethnographers encountered sought to sustain kinship/community networks, even if they embraced modern culture at the expense of the traditional culture of their forebears.

Overcrowding, Homelessness and the Formation of The Block

Before the Housing Commission started to accommodate large numbers of Indigenous tenants in the early 1970s, Aboriginal people in Sydney generally had little choice but to live in overcrowded inner-city terraces. Racist real-estate agents and landlords in middle-class neighbourhoods ensured that few of those who identified or were identifiable as Indigenous were able to obtain rental accommodation outside of the 'black ghetto' areas. Chair of the Royal Australian Institute of Architects, Ian McKay, published the results of a study in which he estimated that 80 per cent of Sydney's Aboriginal population – around 8000 people – needed rehousing (MacKay 1968). He observed that in one house in Georgina Street, Newtown, 13 people lived in one room with a shared kitchen. The study found that throughout New South Wales only 46 per cent of Aboriginal dwellings had kitchens and that only 57 per cent had electricity. Chicka Dixon said:

> [b]ecause Aboriginal people in Sydney have nowhere to stay, they go into areas where they have relatives. I'm no exception. If some of my people come from Wallaga Lake, I put them up. Where else have they got to go? If I haven't a bed they sleep on the floor. They sleep anywhere. I have had up to fifteen or twenty sleeping in my house ... Georgina Street ... is referred to as the Georgina Street Mission, there's so many black people there (Tatz 1975, p. 33).

Beasley found that 57 per cent of the houses that she surveyed had more than two residents per room (where all rooms were counted, including laundry). She also found twice the number of people per dwelling as for the metropolitan population as a whole (Beasley 1970, pp. 157–163).

In spite of the movement of many Aboriginal people into modern suburban housing from the late sixties the problems of overcrowding and poverty endured. One study conducted in 1972 investigated 778 (of what the authors estimated to be 1850) Aboriginal households in Sydney. Of these 22 per cent were in New South Wales Housing Commission or other government homes, 40 per cent in private houses, 20 per cent in self-contained flats and 15 per cent in rooms or non self-contained flats (Scott 1973). It found that more than 500 of those surveyed had no hot running water in the bathroom, that 400 shared a bathroom with another household or had none at all and that 275 households shared or had no kitchen at all. Those without these facilities would not have been Housing Commission dwellings. The living conditions of those in non-government housing were, therefore, particularly overcrowded and poor. Lovejoy estimated in 1971 that there was a backlog of 1100 houses that would need to be constructed in New South Wales to meet Aboriginal housing needs across the state (Lovejoy 1971, p. 85). A considerable proportion of these was required to redress the situation in Sydney.

In addition to those who were housed in inner-city slums there were numerous Aboriginal people, largely single men, who were effectively homeless. Many of them were alcoholics. Brindle wrote of these 'long grass' people:

> When an Aborigine is able to gain the lease of a house he is immediately swamped by relatives. This he doesn't mind. Many are already sleeping in condemned houses awaiting demolition by the Housing Commission, while others sleep in old cars. A large percentage rent shabby little rooms, and late at night sneak their mates in (Brindle 1970).

In 1973 Aboriginal activists and supportive local priests conducted a campaign to counteract the problem of homelessness in Redfern. This led in 1973 to the federal Labor government purchasing a section of terraced housing around Everleigh Street, that later became known as The Block. It was allocated for Aboriginal housing and was eventually owned and managed by the Aboriginal Housing Company (AHC) (Anderson 1993, 2000). The move provoked considerable resistance amongst the local (mainly working-class) residents, 226 of who petitioned local councillors and federal politicians to:

> [C]ondemn the establishment of the ghetto in Louis and Caroline Streets by the Aboriginals who have squatted in these properties . . . We want the Aboriginal ghetto stopped now – for if allowed to continue it will spread plague like throughout the entire South Sydney area (Anderson, K 1993a, p. 328).

The language of contagion, so redolent of nineteenth-century discourses on urban life, resurfaced here in the heat of local conflict. In a letter to the *South Sydney Advertiser* on 17 March 1973, the South Sydney Residents Protection Movement advocated the salt and pepper assimilation that the Housing Commission was already practising in its suburban housing programme because they:

did not want one race or creed confined to one small area as this can only lead to violence and hatred ... So long as persons of different races are distributed evenly–with no large bodies of any one race–they will assimilate with the majority group (Anderson 1993, p. 328).

Notwithstanding resident resistance The Block became the heart of the Indigenous community in Sydney. The original designs for the area embodied utopian aspiration: fences between gardens were to be demolished to produce shared space and communal living. The affairs of The Block were to be run according to the principles of participatory democracy. The vision for the development embodied counter-cultural ideas that were popular amongst young people in this era. Aboriginal activists made links between the alternative lifestyle aspiration for communal living and the social arrangements that prevailed in a traditional Aboriginal setting.

But, like many utopian visions, the plans for The Block went awry. The politics of the Housing Company was later afflicted by a deep and bitter factionalism, with allegations of corruption and nepotism. More destructive however, was the influence of drugs and crime amongst young people. The Block became a centre of drug dealing and addiction amongst young people in the 1980s and '90s, as was sensationally documented in media reports through this period.[9] An Australian Broadcasting Commission *Four Corners* television documentary in 1997 graphically depicted Redfern's heroin subculture and the public discussion that followed resurrected long-held popular fears about slums and inner urban social decay and disorder[10] (Spark 2003). This drug subculture had long been associated with street crime and sporadic violence in the streets of Redfern. The policing of these problems was often heavy-handed and culturally insensitive and, at the low point in the early nineties, the Aboriginal community was locked in a situation of brooding and intractable conflict with the authorities.

In early 2004 violence erupted when a teenage boy, TJ Hickey, died after becoming impaled on a railing after fleeing a police vehicle on his bicycle (Morgan 2004). Local Indigenous people refused to believe police denials that they had been pursuing the boy and fought pitched battles with the riot squad in the streets around Redfern station. Images of the riots appeared on television news bulletins around the world and the area was once again represented as the no-go zone on the edge of Sydney's city centre, and Aboriginal people as deviant and criminals (Gargett 2005). The official position is that Hickey's death was a terrible accident and no charges have been laid in relation to it.

In recent years there has been intense pressure for the renewal of Redfern to enable governments and developers to realise high land values that have long been held down by the stigma associated with The Block. In 2004 the New South Wales government passed a law to establish the Redfern-Waterloo Authority. This move provides the state with greater powers to oversee the redevelopment of the area. The Authority usurps the power of local government, removes the constraints of heritage laws and gives the utilities minister, currently former Lord Mayor of Sydney, Frank Sartor, the ability to compulsorily resume land. He has stated his intention to break down the local concentration of the Aboriginal people largely through the construction of higher density housing with a mixture of social and private dwellings. Sartor argues (in terms reminiscent of Paul Hasluck) that the problems of The Block have less to do with Aboriginality than with the concentration of social disadvantage in one place. The strategy of dispersal is consistent with broader strategies to redevelop and convert public estates in suburban areas with high levels of social disadvantage, to mixed tenure housing. With the publication in early 2006 of the *Redfern Waterloo Plan* the government has sought to restrict the role of the AHC to the administration of a cultural centre and a very small number of Aboriginal-occupied dwellings scattered amongst new mainstream housing.

The AHC, however, has its own agenda. In recent years it has demolished many of The Block's dwellings with most residents moving elsewhere and in 2003 published the *Pemulwuy Plan* (Aboriginal Housing Company 2003). This proposes that the AHC retain control of The Block and oversee the construction of new Aboriginal housing with adjacent cultural facilities. It accepts there should be some private dwellings in the new development but envisages that Indigenous owner-occupiers will take these up. Unlike the state government proposals if the *Pemulwuy Plan* were to be implemented it would retain the character of The Block as a distinctive Indigenous precinct and – unlike what is being proposed by the state government – help to sustain the local cultural attachments. This would stymie the designs of private developers for the symbolic reconstruction of

Redfern – a place that has become almost a metonym for Aboriginal Sydney – and would frustrate the broader ideological intention to make a familiar place once again alien to Indigenous people (Gelder and Jacobs 1998). The current government plans form part of a long history of colonial and modernist reconstructions of space to erase those aspects of Aboriginality that are most threatening. The spectre of the fringe dweller continues to loom large.

In spite of its central and notorious place in the popular imaginary, Redfern and the nearby areas of inner Sydney (and the comparable districts of other large cities), housed a declining proportion of the Aboriginal urban population from the 1960s. The establishment of the government housing program, Housing for Aborigines (HFA), in New South Wales (and comparable schemes elsewhere) produced a huge growth in the numbers of Aboriginal people living in suburban areas. Today, the great majority of Aboriginal urban dwellers live outside the inner city. Their experiences will be explored in chapters 4 and 5.

Pan-Aboriginality and Contemporary Cultural Process

We have seen how most public representations of Aboriginal people in cities cast them as a disruptive and transgressive presence within what was essentially civilised space. Behind the fulminations of moral entrepreneurs and the shocking headlines of the tabloid press, however, was the emergence of a counter-colonial movement. Those who moved to the cities had relinquished the everyday contact with the lands that had traditionally provided them with the coordinates for life. They faced a struggle to anchor their social identities. Rather than giving in to the pressures to assimilate, the diasporic Indigenous peoples who settled in places like Sydney's Redfern formed new networks. They developed a pan-Aboriginal culture and politics that made the Aboriginal rights movement a subversive and powerful presence in public life in the last three decades of the twentieth century. City dwellers, especially young people, defied both official expectations and the poor, overcrowded living conditions they experienced, to develop a new urban Indigenous vernacular.

Far from undergoing a depletion of their Aboriginality with the transition from bush to city, as some urban ethnographers suggested, Indigenous people were involved in an ongoing process of cultural production combining the old and the new, the traditional and the modern (Anderson 1995). Aboriginal people did not eschew ties to communities of origin but built broader forms of association than would have been possible had they remained in the bush. I will argue in Chapter 6 that in spite of this cultural innovation, Aboriginality is still *publicly* defined in predominantly traditional terms. However, grass-roots cultural innovation was taking place beneath these public representations.

As with the formation of working-class solidarity in the new industrial towns, the congregation of Indigenous peoples from different regions in high-density population centres, produced new solidarities. Those who came from small country towns or remote areas were able to relate their particular localised experiences to those of other Aboriginal people who came from elsewhere. Solidarity was built on a realisation that what had happened on the reserve was not peculiar but was part of a more generalised set of experiences. This led to the emergence of a radical pan-Aboriginal politics and associated cultural forms. In inner Sydney in the 1960s and early 1970s, for example, a number of new Aboriginal organisations were set up. These included cultural initiatives like the Black Theatre, sporting groups like the All Blacks football team, and community bodies such as the Aboriginal Medical Service and the Aboriginal Legal Service, which grew into large state-funded organisations. Later, the urban Lands Councils became central in sustaining Indigenous community. Aboriginal politician Linda Burney observed in 2004 that '[t]he Redfern-Waterloo area is truly the birthplace of self-determination in Australia' (New South Wales Parliamentary Standing Committee on Social Issues 2004, p. 165).

Broad Indigenous solidarity was not, however, achieved immediately nor always smoothly. There were considerable divisions within urban Aboriginal populations by region of origin.[11] This often involved a distinct pecking order. Barwick, for example, describes the people who originated from the reserve at Cummeragunga mission in New South Wales and who had moved into Victoria after the strike there in the 1920s as of the highest class amongst the Melbourne Kooris. They took a central role in collective political affairs. Also those from the Western District considered themselves to be superior to the 'station people' from Gippsland (Barwick 1962, p. 21). Inglis also found that the Adelaide Aboriginal population was divided according to which reserve its members originated from (Inglis 1961). Those who hailed from Point Pearce, a profitable and relatively prosperous reserve, 'looked down on' those who came from Port McLeay, a more impoverished place where, although its inhabitants had retained more of their traditional ways, they were less capable farmers. Inglis contends that those who came from Kooniba Mission were held in even lower regard by those from both of the other major reserves. These divisions appeared to matter less among younger people in the cities than their parents' generation. They congregated in pubs and clubs and they were less wedded to the bush than to the city. Barwick argued that with the passage of time, new forms of interaction shaped a 'blackfellow orientation' which cut across what were previously important divisions by social status and region (p. 23).

The orientation developed in a manner similar to the pan-African consciousness that emerged among black students living in Paris in the middle of this century. Among those drawn from far-flung parts of the French Empire were Franz Fanon, who became a theorist of race and colonialism, and poet and cultural theorist Leopold Sedar Senghor, who later became president of Senegal. The idea that migrants to the colonial metropolitan centres from different parts of the world might share a common identity, only became apparent to them as they became the focus of the insults and prejudice of others. Fanon describes walking in the street and being pointed at by a child who cried out 'Look a Negro' to his mother:

> I was responsible at the same time for my body, for my race, for my ancestors. I subjected myself to an objective examination, I discovered my blackness, my ethnic characteristics; and I was battered down by tom toms, cannibalism, intellectual deficiency, fetishism, racial defects, slave-ships ... On that day, completely dislocated, unable to be abroad with the other, the white man, who unmercifully imprisoned me, I took myself far off from my own presence, far indeed and made myself an object (Fanon 1967, p. 112).

Senghor, too, said that it was only on going to Paris that he became conscious of himself as Negro (Howe 1998, p. 26). Yet for all that immigrant groups were classed as one under the colonial gaze, this did not overcome the suspicions and divisions that characterised the relationships between them.

It is unlikely that the sense of existential crisis confronted by Aboriginal people who moved to the cities after World War Two would have been as severe as that described by Fanon. Young Aboriginal people, by contrast with the African students, had come from towns where they were already part of a dominated minority, albeit a larger one than in the city. Nevertheless they, like the Africans, would have felt something of the sense of dislocation which Fanon describes in such powerful terms. The semiotic violence associated with urban life weakened the residual attachments to kin and homeland and made it possible to feel part of a broader diasporic grouping. The pan-African political movement that emerged in these post-colonial circumstances was about re-bonding those whose ancestors had been forcibly removed from their homelands. Yet paradoxically, like pan-Aboriginality, the idea of pan-Africanism presupposes a unity that was never there in the first place. Africa, like other parts of the colonised world, contained diverse and variegated cultural groupings. Such movements, far from involving the reclamation of lost community, are actually about building contemporary politics and culture that draw on histories of oppression. Pan-Aboriginality provided a point of anchorage to many of those city dwellers living away from their home country and popularly viewed as out of place living in the city. They were, as a result, vulnerable to the inference that their Indigenous identities were weakened as a consequence. Pan-Aboriginality made them less foreigners living on the traditional land of another people and more brothers and sisters whose own people had shared something of what had happened there.

In the late 1960s and early '70s, a radical Indigenous movement emerged inspired by the Black Power movement in the United States and committed to breaking with the earlier forms of Aboriginal politics. In place of the liberal 'progress' model, whereby Indigenous representatives collaborated with sympathetic whitefellas, the young leadership took up the cause of self-determination. Rather than lobbying and petitioning parliamentarians – the politics of the cautious older generation – they embraced the revolutionary culture and direct action that were being promoted by student groups around the world at this time. Chicka Dixon recalled in the mid 1970s that he had warned the federal government about the volatile situation which existed in the inner cities with the arrival of young people emboldened by radical politics:

> If we keep crowding them into this sort of area, it will develop into something similar to Harlem and the black ghettoes. The same thing is happening in Sydney, and there is an explosion point coming. If nothing is done about the situation, then it's quite certain that there are going to be race riots (Tatz 1975, p. 34).

Although he was supportive of this new spirit of self-determination, Dixon was aware that as a small minority, any violent action by Aboriginal activists could harm their cause. His plea was for public funding to ameliorate the living conditions of Indigenous city dwellers.

A process of ethnogenesis accompanied the emergence of this new politics: the construction of public symbolic forms geared to unifying a hitherto fragmented and diverse group (Jones and Hill-Burnett 1992). These symbols were often primordial, drawing on or referring to traditional culture and suggesting an ancient Aboriginality. This concealed the fact that the social and political process of building a broad Indigenous movement was a contemporary one, that the people living in cities were engaged in developing collective culture considerably different from the traditional forms. Although the actions of Aboriginal activists around this time received much media coverage – most famously with the establishment of a Tent Embassy outside Parliament House in Canberra in 1972 – there was nevertheless considerable disquiet amongst those so-called 'cultural blacks' who lived away from the cities and mistrusted urban radicals. Many of these people, particularly in remote areas, viewed Aboriginal city-dwellers as lacking authenticity and some were resentful of the appropriation of particular local symbols for the Aboriginal movement as a whole. Some were fearful that Black Power urban radicalism would produce a backlash in the bush and were much more at ease with a gradualist politics (Gilbert 1977). Chicka Dixon stated:

> They say 'You oldies, you squares, you cop this, you bow your head to the white man. We won't bow our heads'. Right now in Sydney there are groups who are advocating Black Power, they're reading literature from the Negro people, they're wearing soul brother and soul sister shirts, they're combing their hair up in Afro style, and they're shaking clenched fists. Now this can be prevented (Tatz 1975, p. 34).

Notwithstanding these divisions (which are less pronounced today than they were) the Aboriginal rights movement produced a thorough attack on residual colonialism and laid the foundation for the contemporary critique of Australian history and social, cultural and political life.

Conclusion

We saw in Chapter 1 how the process of building settler colonies involves erasing the traces of prior Indigenous presence. By the twentieth century in Australia's large cities Aboriginality had been rendered strange and deviant.

Chapter 2 showed how Aboriginal affairs, particularly in the era of assimilation, constituted the boundaries of cities and towns as the threshold between the old life and the new. Those who crossed had, in the official point of view, tacitly accepted the obligation to modernise and jettison their cultural baggage.

This chapter has shown that Aboriginal people rejected the terms of this contract and the destinies that were mapped out for them. Most of those who were pushed or pulled towards the poor areas of the inners cities in the twentieth century wished to sustain communal ties and did so. Those who made this journey found that the way they were perceived was also shaped by broader ideological structures and social tensions that had their roots in Victorian cities. The town planning movement emerged because the middle classes believed the urban masses posed a threat to social order. The urban reformers believed that by redesigning their living places the poor they would be encouraged to practise a respectable way of life. Such environmental determinism was at the basis of the twentieth-century slum clearance campaigns and, as we shall see in the next chapter, shaped the moral economy of suburban life. The general concern about Aboriginal neighbourhoods echoed American (and international) concerns about black ghettos like Harlem in New York. Not only were the slum dwellers poor, unemployed and likely to turn to crime and immoral habits of all sorts, they were also black. Aboriginal people in inner Sydney presented a paradox. They constituted a resistant sub-culture and signified that Aboriginality was dynamic and adaptable. They belied the thesis of cultural loss and demonstrated the emergence of a new national Indigenous politics and culture. Pan-Aboriginality drew on tradition but it also overturned the parochialism that had long characterised Indigenous life. It lent a new resistant and organised political face to Aboriginality and, most importantly, provided a sense of anchorage for those who were away from their home country and community.

Chapter 4

Suburban Dreaming

> My first glimpse of the house left me with a lump in my throat. When the kids asked why I was crying I said they were happy tears. We hugged each other and then the big job of moving in began. It was a four bedroom house with a front porch … I found out that you were not supposed to create a nuisance or disturb any of the neighbours. You weren't able to have anyone come and stay without permission from the Commission. It reminded me of the missions. The rule was useless in our culture where survival often depended on being able to stay with friends and relatives (Langford 1988, pp. 173–174).

The 1960s was a key decade in the history of colonial relations. In the period since the establishment of reserves in the mid-nineteenth century, the state had largely sought to separate Indigenous people and their culture from European society. Their living places were segregated from those of towns-folk, and their social welfare needs were dealt with in a quarantined field of public administration. But these policy strategies were being undermined by the movement of Aboriginal people to urban areas and by the growth in the numbers of those living outside the reserve system. The 1967 referendum vote, which had the effect of extending Aboriginal rights, reflected a waning in post-war conservatism and indicated that public opinion had shifted away from the idea that Indigenous people were outside the imagined community of nation. The brazenly racist rhetoric that was a routine feature of the public sphere in the past receded during the sixties as discussion of Aboriginal affairs was couched in more liberal terms. There was a growing acceptance in public debate that the conditions of life of the nation's original inhabitants should be measured against the same yardsticks as were applied to other citizens. Such discourses, however, by no means spelled an end to official racism. Aboriginal people continued to suffer scrutiny and regulation of their culture and way of life, albeit from different bureaucracies.

In New South Wales, the *Aborigines Act 1969*, dissolved the AWB and transferred responsibility for Indigenous affairs to mainstream government departments. The New South Wales Housing Commission took over responsibility for Indigenous housing and the government introduced the Housing for Aborigines (HFA) scheme. This earmarked a portion of public housing for Indigenous people, and was accompanied by progressive rhetoric about moving Aboriginal people from government reserves and unofficial camps and into the social mainstream. Yet the process was far from satisfactory because the number of houses was insufficient to overcome the shortage caused by earlier governmental neglect. In order to be among the few offered houses Indigenous applicants had to demonstrate their suitability for life in the new environment. They were expected to embrace a lifestyle which was at odds with their culture and traditional way of life; to live in dwellings designed for 'respectable' nuclear families and weaken ties to their extended kinship and community networks. Some conformed but many of those who wished for improved housing were unwilling to make the sacrifices required of them.

The New South Wales Housing Commission

The Housing Commission was set up in 1942 with the long-term aim of providing affordable housing for low-income people. Under the Commonwealth State Housing Agreement of 1945 the Commonwealth Government provided funds for public housing. This led to a construction programme of unprecedented scale such that approximately one third of dwellings built up to 1960 were financed by federal and state governments (Greig 1995, p. 36). This pattern continued in the sixties. In New South Wales much of the new housing was constructed on broad-acre suburban estates under the auspices of the Housing Commission. These included vast developments in Sydney like those at Green Valley, Mt Druitt and Campbelltown, parts of the central coast and many of the developments on the fringes of country towns.

These were not, however, simply places to accommodate the population overflow of post-war Australia. They were also social laboratories, part of a modernist reconstruction of urban space (Peel 1995). The state sought to design environments conducive to producing good citizens for a young growing nation. Prospective tenants from all social backgrounds – Anglo working class, migrant, Indigenous – had to present themselves as worthy. They had to demonstrate they were capable of living in a manner deemed respectable by those petty officials who exercised the power to grant or refuse them a place on the waiting list. After each aspiring tenant had lodged their application a Commission officer was sent out to inspect the dwelling in which the applicant family lived. Eligible applicants were vetted according to need. It is in the determination of this need that the ideological complexion of the post-war public housing programme was revealed. Housing Commission officers had considerable discretionary powers in assessing applicants' suitability for housing. Those seeking housing firstly had to show that they were not adequately accommodated where they were. Factors taken into account included overcrowding and whether the dwelling was habitable and in an adequate state of repair. They also had to demonstrate they were capable of meeting the Commission standards in the areas of 'civic pride' (in maintaining the exterior of the dwelling and the garden), neighbourliness, living a modest and respectable domestic life and ability to meet regular rental payments.

The Housing Commission Tenancy Files (including HFA or 'Special Tenancy' [ST] files[1]) contain the reports and notes written by the Housing Commission officers expressing opinions on the merits and shortcomings of applicants and tenants. They reflected the prevailing view that no individual or group had the *right* to public housing. Although by the 1960s the ethos of social democracy and the welfare state was firmly in place, the day-to-day operation of the Housing Commission was more in keeping with the character of the pre-war modernist state. Officials sifted out the deserving from the undeserving poor and policed the lifestyle and culture of those who were lucky enough to get past the gatekeepers. The sort of information which is contained on files, therefore, goes beyond the routine paperwork which one might expect in a system whereby resources are allocated based on rights enjoyed by certain categories of people.

The Housing for Aborigines Programme

In theory Aboriginal people had been eligible to apply for public housing since the inception of the Housing Commission in 1942. Very few, however, did so (Joint Committee 1967, p. 31). Aboriginal people in general did not trust state authority and were reluctant to put themselves forward. Many were also presumably ignorant of their right to apply or baffled by the procedures of the Commission. Those who were able to surmount these obstacles and complete the application forms were rarely successful. They generally lived in conditions of extreme poverty and were deemed by Housing Commission inspectors to be unlikely to assimilate to the required cultural and community standards. The prevalent view that Aboriginal people did not belong in cities or towns, much less in government housing, is reflected in the comments of one inspector assessing an application for housing from an Aboriginal family in the late 1940s:

> These people are Aboriginals. There is another baby on the way since the application was filled in there are now seven people sleeping in one room. I could not make any rec. other than bad. They should have better conditions but not as tenants of the Commission.[2] (Inspector's emphasis ST 2374 Box 10/41266)
>
> Few Aboriginal people applied before 1960.

From this date, however, public policy moved in a more progressive direction. Despite Housing Commission Chair Purcell arguing that most Indigenous people were not ready for town housing, the 1967 Joint New South Wales Parliamentary Committee into Aboriginal Welfare recommended that the aim of integration would be best served through the creation of a separate pool of suburban housing for Indigenous people. The Committee's report stated that 'the congregation (and isolation) of Aboriginals on reserves is one of the main factors retarding them from becoming full members of the community' (Joint Committee 1967, Part 1, p. 19).

The *Aborigines Act* was passed by the New South Wales parliament in February 1969 with bipartisan support and calls for community tolerance.[3] It reflected similar changes that were taking place in other Australian states at the time. Liberal government minister, Willis, stated that 'in life's various situations … the fitness and personal decision of the individual alone are to count without any reference to colour or ancestry' (p. 3725). Behind these noble sentiments, however, lay fiscal motivations. Willis alluded to huge rental arrears for reserve housing that the AWB had been unable to recover (p. 3726). The Housing Commission was thought likely to be a more officious landlord, less prone to the paternalism practised by the Board. The Opposition Labor Party applauded the moves towards mainstreaming including in the area of housing. Its spokesperson said the AWB 'has existed for a long time but overall it has been a failure. However … its work was largely hampered by political apathy on both sides of the House … Parliament … did not give it the money or the wherewithal to do the job that it could have done' (pp. 3740–3741).

The Housing Commission initiated the HFA programme in 1969 pursuant to the legislative changes and began to build and purchase houses mainly in areas where pre-existing construction and development was taking place.[4] The administrative procedures and selection criteria were similar to those prevailing in the mainstream housing programme so that even after the scheme was introduced many of those who were poor and had little education had only remote prospects of obtaining housing.[5] While most Aboriginal people could demonstrate that they had a need for public housing, very few were willing or able to demonstrate the requisite moral conformity. Only families with children were eligible to apply for public housing, or pensioners seeking specifically designated aged-person units. Single people and childless couples were excluded from Commission dwellings.[6]

In the period 1970–1975 many Aboriginal people moved into government housing. As of mid 1975:

> 1231 dwellings [were] occupied by Aboriginal families … Of this number 575 had been constructed by the Housing Commission since 1969 (Letter from Minister for Housing LF McGinty 2 October 1975 ST 4225 Box 14/1413).[7]

At this time there were 735 Aboriginal families whose names had been approved from admission to the waiting lists and a further 438 applications were being processed. The construction programme had reached a peak of 300 the previous year. This was cut down to 150 for 1975–1976.

Despite all this, large numbers of Aboriginal people continued to be inadequately housed especially those in remote areas. McKay's 1968 study had concluded that, throughout New South Wales 78 per cent of the Indigenous population was in need of new housing (McKay 1968). The 1971 census showed that 20 per cent of Aboriginal people in New South Wales continued to live in improvised dwellings – sheds, tents, garages or humpies – particularly in the far west[8] (Henderson 1975, p. 263). A medical delegation, led by Professor Fred Hollows, lobbied the federal government in 1974 arguing that '922 houses were required for 1000 needy families in more than 50 NSW country areas'. They contended that many of the epidemics of Third World diseases that were experienced by Aboriginal communities could be alleviated with the provision of better housing (*Sydney Morning Herald* 18 September 1974, p. 2).

Urbanisation and the Aboriginal Family Resettlement Scheme

The HFA programme helped to accelerate a trend of urbanising the New South Wales Indigenous population that had been apparent since World War Two. Between 1971 and '91 the proportion of the Aboriginal people living in major urban areas (Sydney, Newcastle and Wollongong) rose from 27.4 to 37.7 per cent. Those living in towns with more than 5000 residents rose from 39.4 to 44.4 per cent while there was an almost 50 per cent reduction in the proportion of New South Wales Indigenous residents living in rural areas – 33.2 to 17.9 per cent (Burnley 1996, p. 12). Both the welfare and housing bureaucracies sought to persuade Indigenous people to move to population centres where most new Housing Commission dwellings were being built. However, only a minority of the applicants who moved to Sydney to take up Commission housing came directly from country areas. The majority were already living in the inner city at the time of application (Legislative Committee 1981, Section 7). HFA, therefore, also had the effect of shifting large numbers of Indigenous city dwellers from private to public tenancies.

There was also, however, a strong regional emphasis in the housing programme. In the early 1970s the Commission constructed and acquired HFA houses in larger country centres like Wagga Wagga, Nowra, Tamworth, Kempsey, Armidale and Dubbo. Applicants for housing had to nominate the Commission zone in which they wished to reside. In some areas such as the far west of New South Wales there was little Commission housing. Applicants had to wait years for housing in towns such as Bourke, Brewarrina, Menindee, Wilcannia and Condoblin. In order to obtain better housing in a reasonable time they had to move to larger towns.

Some moved to regional centres where employment prospects were better, under the Aboriginal Family Resettlement Scheme. This scheme was jointly funded by the federal and state governments and provided successful applicants with intensive counselling support when they arrived at their new locations. Many Aboriginal people were relocated from places in the far west and north west of the state that already had declining populations and opportunities to towns like Newcastle, Orange, Albury, Wagga Wagga, Tamworth and Cobar. The general pattern was that all of those who came from one area were relocated together. Bourke and Brewarrina people went to Newcastle, those from Wilcannia to Albury, those from Lake Cargelligo and West Wyalong to Wagga and those from Moree and Bogabilla to Tamworth.

Whether the Resettlement Scheme was yet another episode in the sorry history of forced relocation or whether it met the legitimate aspirations of Aboriginal people for better houses and better lives is not clear. It clearly served further to weaken attachment to traditional land. Goodall suggests that many community leaders, frequently those who already had good housing, were enticed to resettle as part of a strategy of encouraging chain migration and that many people applied under duress (Goodall 1996, p. 334). Isabelle McLeod, who had been one of the first Aboriginal people resettled by the Board in Western Sydney, was the secretary of the Family Resettlement Corporation and wrote a short book about the scheme which was published in 1982 (McLeod 1982). She defended the scheme against its critics, arguing that it was largely controlled by Aboriginal people (Chicka Dixon was foundation chair) and that the support which tenants received in their new locations included placing them in contact with Aboriginal organisations. However, the 'counselling' which was offered clearly extended and complemented the assimilation and social control regimes that formed part of the operation of the Housing Commission:

> Through resettlement many women become involved in committees and take an active part in organising sewing, cooking and craft classes. There was not much chance to learn these skills on the riverbank (McLeod 1982, p. 35).

There is also evidence that those who moved to new locations under the scheme encountered the resentment of local Aboriginal people (Legislative Committee 1981, Section 7). This was because the migrants received priority over locals on the HFA waiting lists and financial assistance for furniture that was not available to others.

Of the approximately 200 families resettled, around a quarter returned to their hometowns (McLeod 1982, p. 49). These figures may not be much higher than would apply to those who moved to cities or towns in other ways. A doctoral study into the psychological aspects of resettlement programmes yielded ample evidence of its shortcomings (Mitchell 1978). By the mid seventies, many of the job opportunities that had been promised in the destination cities and towns had disappeared. The global recession of the time created higher unemployment levels in the general population and Aboriginal people were among the least likely to be employed. A Legislative Committee of the New South Wales parliament in 1981 was told of the disastrous experience of those who relocated from Moree to the larger town of Tamworth in the late seventies, many of whom gave up employment to do so, but were unable to find jobs in their new homes. The scheme wound up in the early 1980s when it was found to be not meeting its objectives.

The Administration of Aboriginal Housing

After the initial application for Housing Commission/HFA tenancy was lodged a Commission inspector was sent out to inspect the dwelling in which the applicant family lived, to assess both need and suitability.[9] In some country towns Housing Application Committees oversaw the recommendations of inspectors on who should be offered Commission housing. These bodies – which covered mainstream as well as Aboriginal applicants –

were made up of four people: a representative from local government, one returned serviceman, one from the local Country Women's Association and one nominated by the local state Member of Parliament. Although the committees generally accepted the recommendations of the inspectors (there was rarely evidence to the contrary in the Special Tenancy files), they nevertheless reinforced the operation of conservative assimilationist values in their oversight of the allocation process. Until 1981 there was no identified Aboriginal representation on housing committees to address the particular needs of Indigenous people. This meant, amongst other things, that decisions on where to site HFA houses were made without reference to the communities whose members could expect to be accommodated there.

Housing Commission officers assessed applicants and recommended which of them should be granted housing. Many asked members of the white community about applicants' suitability and wrote notes about these conversations on the housing files. Little regard was paid to applicants' privacy. Welfare and charity establishments, real-estate agents, employers and, in some cases, even neighbours were consulted. Most were inclined to make instant moral (usually racist) judgements, some of which were misinformed and based on rumour. It was very common, especially in the country, for inspectors to approach the local police about an applicant's suitability. MS, a single father of three children, was refused accommodation on the grounds that 'he has served a jail term for assault', even though the incident had taken place several years previously. He made a subsequent successful application and was a good tenant (ST 7347 Box 14/1415). When a single mother applied for housing in Broken Hill a Housing Commission inspector visited the house where she was living, only to find her not at home (ST 3426 Box 14/1414). He then proceeded to the local police station where he was told that the applicant was 'in and out of the local lockup with frequent charges of drunkenness as a result of nights out with various male friends'. She was refused accommodation. The Armidale district officer consulted the Walcha police about the character of applicant BN (ST 3698 Box 14/1413). The officer asked about both his police record and his attitude to work. The police also volunteered information about his domestic life. They provided a surveillance function the purpose of which went beyond the maintenance of law and order.

The Housing Commission officer who investigated SR's application for a mainstream Commission house in Sydney, found the family living in temporary accommodation and saw fit to consult a real-estate agent responsible for the flat which the R family had previously occupied (ST 4208 Box 14/1413). In the conversation (8 October 1968):

> Mr [W] said the premises were left in an indescribable mess. He said it was utterly filthy and 'it was very poor even for an Aboriginal'. He stated that there were Aboriginals coming to and from the premises all the time to participate in 'drinking parties'. He said 'take it from me don't touch him with a forty foot pole–he's trouble. It would be a gross injustice to even contemplate housing such a person'.

In 1975 when he applied again, SR and his family were highly recommended for housing and found to have very high standards of cleanliness and housekeeping. These examples illustrate the power which Commission officers had, particularly outside of large cities where local information could trap people in reputations which they found hard to shake off. The demeaning prospect of having their personal lives raked over by the 'long socks' (Aboriginal term for minor bureaucrats) would undoubtedly have deterred many people from applying for Commission housing.

Compliance and Resistance

A leaflet published by the Federated Council for the Advancement of Aborigines and Torres Strait Islanders (FCAATSI) in the early 1970s entitled *How to Play the Housing Game in New South Wales: Rules for Aboriginal Players* advised applicants that to prepare for the visit of a housing officer:

> Ideally all beds should be made, all eating utensils washed up, and the house should smell fresh and clean. Food scraps left lying around to attract vermin, or the house smelling dirty will upset the Housing Commission. If you do not have a regular garbage service, you should have collected all the rubbish together tidily and burnt it. Every home should have a toilet and it should also smell clean (Records of FCAATSI, Mitchell Library: MLMSS 2999 318 Y601).

Commission officers visited applicants' dwellings in order to scan them for signs of respectability. Their aim was to pluck promising applicants from lives of poverty and to encourage them into respectable suburban habits – regular work patterns and stable, clean and virtuous nuclear family life where they maintained their dwellings and were considerate of neighbours. The officers expected to be received as guests with the house tidied and presented in *Home Beautiful* fashion and tea served. These inspections were akin to the demeaning home inspections that reserve dwellers had to endure. It made little difference to Aboriginal people whether it was the reserve manager, his wife or a Housing Commission inspector who came. The purpose of the visit was always to monitor progress towards assimilation.

It is impossible to generalise about the ways in which Aboriginal applicants responded to this assessment process. The archives contain both examples of those who clearly took trouble to present themselves as eager and respectable and of those who made little effort to conform. The former made their dwellings appear neat and as clean as possible and perhaps dressed their children in best clothes. The considerable demand for public housing indicated that many Aboriginal people, particularly women, were anxious to enjoy the better living conditions which suburban housing would bring them, yet this did not in itself imply a readiness to comply with the cultural expectations.

Some applicants already lived in a manner that matched the requirements of the Commission. A Housing Commission inspector described SD as 'a good little housewife and mother' based on his superficial inspection of her home (ST 3422 Box 14/1414). People such as these made the transition from reserve or rental accommodation with few problems. Most, however, did not. Some of this group were aware of what was required of them and put on their best face on the day of inspection. Numerous applicants who received glowing assessments, incurred the wrath of neighbours and Commission officers once they had taken up occupancy, for not complying with 'community' standards.

Many, however, encountered the inspecting officers without having prepared themselves and their living spaces in a manner likely to meet approval. If they believed that their chances were improved by inspecting officers taking pity on their obvious poverty, they were wrong. Only those who had put up the best appearance were judged capable of assimilating to suburban life and admitted to the waiting list. Even if they wanted to, it was difficult for Aboriginal people to fabricate the appearance of nuclear family harmony and order both because they were poor and because they often had relatives staying with them and lots of children around. The inspection process, therefore, presented many applicants with a dilemma. To exclude family was to signal a willingness to weaken social bonds. Most embraced the mutual and gregarious traditions of community and were not prepared to conceal these attachments to their people. They brought a take-me-as-you-find-me approach to the evaluation process. Even though this was apparently self-defeating, it signified not simply a localised knee-jerk resistance to white authority, but a desire to hold onto the cultural, if not the material, conditions of life they were used to.

The HFA tenancy files indicate that direct angry exchanges occurred during the inspection process. On rare occasions the file notes described resistance that was framed in terms of collective Aboriginal political demands for land. For example the file of MH (ST 1464 Box 14/1457) contains a memo which referred to her partner and his family in the following terms:

> Both RG and his parents are very difficult to deal with and antagonistic to anyone in authority. On 6 December 1973 he went on with a great tirade about how Aboriginal people are being discriminated against and in particular how the Summervale Reserve was now only a small proportion of the original ... his defacto wife supported him ... [they] did not impress favourably.

Goodall argues that it is important to connect the movement for town housing through the Housing Commission to a broader politics of land rights (Goodall 1986, Chapter 21–22). The effect of this is not particularly noticeable in the tenancy files. But this is probably a consequence of Commission officers misrepresenting the nature of applicants' challenges to them, such as to omit references, for instance, to the excision of reserve land as a factor leading to applications for town housing. Most of those who applied for government housing had long experience of domineering officialdom and were probably reluctant to engage in obstreperous political confrontation. The desire for land rights was almost certainly the sub text to many assessment encounters.

Class and Gender in the Assessment Process

Although racist judgements were commonly made of Aboriginal applicants, class and gender evaluations were also central to the inspection process. The invigilation of domestic and family life, although laden with ethnocentric cultural norms, cannot simply be reduced to colonial relations. The general mission of the Housing Commission was to identify the deserving poor: those who, given the opportunity, would escape the bad influences of their environment – principally in regard to non Indigenous applicants, the crime and other social problems of inner-city slum areas – and pursue social mobility and moral respectability. When the responsibility for Aboriginal housing was transferred to the Housing Commission, Indigenous people were exposed to similar ideological structures.

Housing Commission officers rarely expressed sympathy for applicants' impoverished circumstances but the odd one recorded admiration for the way an applicant was able to defy their living conditions. One who inspected a single parent family living in a private rental property in Sydney wrote:

> v. old 2br brick cottage which is dilapidated and in very poor condition. It is v. damp with roof leaks, collapsed floorboards which have been patched over and only one burner on the stove works. The only means to heat the bath is an old gas copper. Despite the bad conditions she keeps the cottage, children and herself remarkably clean and neat (ST 1967 Box 14/1455).

Generally, however, inspectors were more inclined to see Aboriginal applicants who lived in tiny humpies on reserves or dilapidated overcrowded city terraces as culpable; to blame them for creating their circumstances rather than seeing them as victims. The comments of one who visited a family on a reserve are typical:

> A definite case of gross overcrowding and primative [sic] conditions, no facilities such as water or electricity. Laundry and bathing has to be done

> in the river. Interior very untidy. If allocated a Housing Commission dwelling total neglect of property would occur (ST 1995 Box 14/1453).

One man made numerous applications for housing for his family and all of them were rejected. The Housing Investigation report stated 'Children very dirty. Yard very untidy with carpets etc. No washing or bathing facilities. Could be blamed for some hygiene problems. CHILDREN VERY DIRTY' (ST 3365 Box 14/1414). Their dwelling had 'pit toilet, no bathroom, wash in tub in bedroom. No Laundry.'

Early assessments of Aboriginal applicants, those from the 1940s through to the mid 1960s, were much harsher than those made after the HFA programme was introduced. In the late 1960s and '70s, state and community welfare organisations often lobbied energetically on behalf of Aboriginal applicants. This had a limited impact but welfare considerations were never paramount in the operating procedures of the Commission. Its primary function was to build neat respectable suburban communities, not to ameliorate poverty. In 1972 an inspector wrote of an applicant living outside Kempsey:

> ... the premises are in a shocking state and to expect an increase in the standard of living would be expecting too much of any applicant let alone a not too bright aboriginal applicant (ST 143 Box 10/41265).

Aboriginal husbands and wives often did not share the same level of ambition to obtain housing. The majority of applicants were women and in many instances it was apparent that men applied on behalf of their family at the urging of their partners. Often women attempted to conform to the requirements of the inspection only to be frustrated by the appearance of their husbands who were drunk or who expressed hostility towards the Commission officer:

> ... he came in during the visit. He was obviously under the influence of alcohol–(ST 1997 Box 14/1455).

> app. hopelessly drunk and in a violent mood as I was interviewing his wife. He had just been in a fight and his victim was leaving by taxi. He

> and several drunken males drinking wine and carousing with gins– (ST 2173 Box 14/1424).

These sorts of observations invariably led to a recommendation that the application be rejected regardless of the efforts of the women.

Women were frequently the target of critical moral judgements by Commission officers. File notes often contained a pastiche of class and race as well as gender prejudices. Inspectors expressed stereotypical notions that Aboriginal women were slovenly, promiscuous and neglectful of their children. A 1971 application from a single mother elicited the following assessment:

> MG is almost totally illiterate. She is 23 ... and had four children ... She appears to be a woman of very loose morals and is not sure of the parentage of one of her children ... it is quite obvious that the four children between them have 3 diff. fathers (ST 2147 Box 14/1423).

Another single mother of three living in overcrowded circumstances with her mother in a small town, applied for housing in 1975. The inspector arrived to find her not home but went ahead with the inspection anyway:

> I was shown her room by her mother and found it to be in a very untidy condition. There were food scraps on the floor as well as dirty clothes and food wrappers. Not to mention a Modess [sanitary] pad. The beds were in a very unkept [sic] state (ST 3426 Box 14/1414).

These comments deal not only with untidiness but also with immodesty. The applicant was measured against middle-class standards of femininity. In 1961 a Redfern family sought emergency accommodation after a house fire destroyed many of their belongings and forced them to move in with friends. The inspection report conducted at the friend's house cited overcrowding and 'poorly defined sleeping arrangements' as evidence that the applicant 'is an undesirable person' (ST 1611 Box 10/41265). The Commission viewed the appropriate division of domestic space as a hallmark of moral probity.

Commission officers did not feel obliged to provide preferential treatment to women who sought to escape abusive, dangerous domestic situations. They saw other state and community bodies as responsible for dealing with these situations. The process of allocating housing operated by different rules. GB was living with her husband and four young children in the Housing Commission home of her parents in Mt Druitt (ST 1993 Box 14/1453). She applied for her own house and the assessment report noted:

> Living in a Housing Commission home which is in a filthy run down state. Has had a row with her husband because he fell asleep minding the children while his wife and mother-in-law were at 'housie'. They arrived home to find a bottle of beer beside him and the radiator on. They quarrelled about this provoking G's husband into producing a gun. The police were called in but didn't charge him. Would suggest further investigation to see how Georgina's domestic problems sort themselves out before deciding whether she would be a suitable tenant.

The social-engineering functions of the Commission predominated over any social welfare considerations that might have come to light in the assessment process.

Inspecting officers generally made little allowance for the difficulties that mothers, particularly single mothers, faced in keeping their houses clean and tidy while the children were around. One such woman, eighteen years old with one child and pregnant with a second, applied for housing in 1978. The officer wrote:

> She is in need of housing but the condition of the flat she occupies is far from good. There were stains on the carpet in the lounge room area. The kitchen area floor was sticky when walked upon, food scraps and cooking items, fat etc were on the kitchen benches. The young son's room seemed to be in neat and tidy order considering her stage of pregnancy. Her own bedroom was in an appalling condition. Clothes were lying all over the floor, drink bottles and cups, beds unmade. The whole apartment had a foul odour (ST 5846 Box 10/41238).

Applicants were compared to the ideal type of the capable suburban mother who manages home and family effortlessly.

There is very little reference in the Housing Commission archives to the state removal of children from their parents as a factor in the process of assessing applicants or indeed in the subsequent surveillance and evaluation of tenants. The Commission only catered for those with custody of children. Those without were ineligible to apply. CD had one child living with her and her defacto spouse at Greenhills reserve. The others had been taken away by the AWB. In a letter attached to an application in 1971 she wrote:

> The quicker I received a home here in Kempsey the quicker my children will be returned to my care from the children's homes which they are in. I haven't seen them for twelve months (ST 136 Box 10/41265).

She was refused housing on the grounds that her housekeeping standards were inadequate. The personal agony she experienced as a result of the separation appeared to do little to persuade the Commission to look favourably on her application. One year later she applied again and wrote:

> Two of my children are home and the house is two [sic] small for the other children when they come out of homes. I want to live in town away from the reserve so the children can get a chance to live properly in a home away from the drunks and were [sic] they might not get in to trouble.

The Commission again declined her application but provided her with a larger house on the reserve.

Inspectors not only made comments about the state of applicants' living environments, they felt at liberty to include on their assessment reports remarks on the personal appearance and hygiene of women. Men were rarely subjected to the same form of appraisal. When an officer visited an applicant in Port Kembla in 1969 at midday he found the applicant's wife:

> sweeping in the back garden. She was still clad in her pyjamas and her hair was very untidy. Sleepout occupied by applicant and family also untidy. I cannot recommend from this inspection (ST 1488 Box 14/1457).

Another, in assessing an elderly Aboriginal woman for suitability for an aged-care unit wrote that she:

> has been unbearable to stand near because of her bodily dirtiness and her boisterous manner. Even if Mrs D wears an acceptable frock it is usually worn over dirty undergarments and one wonders if she has ever understood the elementary steps of personal hygiene or laundering of clothes and house linen (ST 1561 Box 14/1457).

It appears that Commission officers felt themselves to be under few constraints when drafting information about applicants' suitability:

> The mother is quite dark, fairly slovenly in dress and appearance and with an unfortunate disfiguring birthmark about the size of a 20c piece on her nose (ST 2898 Box 14/1423).

Women were expected to cultivate a genteel and orderly domestic life to provide a sanctuary for the nuclear family. Commission officers conducting initial inspections took a dim view of the presence of members of the extended family in the household of applicants. They generally saw this as evidence that applicants would be unlikely to live along required family lines if offered housing:

> Very little care given in maintaining the house. Housekeeping standards very poor . . . Mrs B. was involved in a large party [during the interiew] . . . under the influence of alcohol and did not impress as a suitable type . . . This woman is well known as a heavy drinker (ST 4201 Box 14/1413).

Passing, The City and The Commission

For the middle third of the twentieth century, state policies were based on the assumption that Aboriginal people would eventually come to see the superiority of European ways of life and willingly abandon their ties to Aboriginal community and assimilate. Although the HFA scheme provided separate identified housing stock, Housing Commission officers still saw their role as encouraging exemplary applicants to assimilate and even to pass as non Indigenous if they desired. This was possible in some areas, particularly on large city estates, where HFA dwellings were scattered 'salt and pepper' or 'chequerboard' fashion throughout the government estates.

The Housing Commission files demonstrate that:

a) many saw the prospect of Commission housing as a way to escape from their communities and from the cultures of poverty, hopelessness and addiction they had experienced there
b) some of these showed a desire to conceal their Aboriginality from neighbours and other local people, or at least not to divulge the fact that they had Aboriginal family connections, largely to avoid the racism they anticipated would result from their identifying
c) others still did not pass but nevertheless sought to distance themselves from their relatives.

The archival evidence indicates that it is inappropriate to see passing and identifying as dichotomous options for Aboriginal people moving into town housing, particularly during the sixties and seventies. The process was complex involving degrees of concealment and openness, at different times and in different social settings.

Most Commission officers were keen to encourage those who demonstrated house pride, sobriety and steady work habits to break away from their relatives and to play down their Aboriginal cultural identity. One typical file note commented of a single mother applicant from Surry Hills:

> She is favourably known in the district – she is not known to the police – she avoids her few adversely known relatives ... and has risen above her general family standards and she leads a worthwhile and very satisfactory home life (ST 1967 Box 14/1455).

When SD applied on behalf of herself, husband and children in 1974, in an attempt to get away from the Greenhills reserve near Kempsey she was assessed as 'a good little housewife and mother'. However, much of the HFA housing in the town had been concentrated in a single area.[10] In a letter of November that year she wrote:

> We feel we must reject this offer as there are eleven Aboriginal families with from two to eleven children per home. This means we would be

> no further ahead in our aim of privacy and the right to rear our children as individuals (ST 3422 Box 14/1414).

The Commission accepted this as a valid reason for rejecting the house and a second offer was made and rejected on the same grounds. One year later in another letter (29 October 1975) the applicant wrote:

> G and I have decided we are moving to Grafton and would like to transfer our Housing Commission application to this area. We feel we want to get out on our own away from all the relatives.

This attempt to distance the family from the community was partly built on the wish for improvements in material life but partly on the desire to remove children from what their parents perceived as detrimental Aboriginal influences. A similar case is that of the S family who also lived at Greenhills reserve. They applied for town housing in 1973 with six children under the age of nine:

> It was ascertained that they are requesting housing at Port Macquarie not at Kempsey or Sydney ... the family feel that there are less [sic] Aboriginal families in Pt. Mac. and with a big family of children they feel the children will have the opportunity to grow up in a normal community environment in that town (ST 3639 Box 10/4169).

In general it was the parents of young children who expressed this desire to break away. Quite often marriages between non-Indigenous men and Aboriginal women led to a form of passing, particularly in cities and large towns. C recalls her family being visited by an aunt from Nowra when she was young.[11] The aunt identified another Aboriginal woman, a distant relative, living in the street. This woman had not previously disclosed her Aboriginality. She was married to a man of Anglo background but later became very close to C's family and was from that point prepared openly to identify. In 1973, RS, a 23-year-old non Indigenous man living in Sydney, applied on behalf of himself, his Aboriginal wife and baby. The inspection report noted:

> Suitable. Wife of applicant predominantly aborigine and wishes to apply under the HFA program but does not wish to be housed in an aboriginal community (ST 3390 Box 10/41267).

The concealment of Aboriginality was apparently much less common (in the more unusual circumstances) where Aboriginal men married non-Indigenous women.

The ultimate aim of government housing policies was to encourage tenants to move eventually into home ownership. Very few Aboriginal families followed this path. An exception was the L family from Sydney. Their initial application was lodged while RL, her husband D and two children lived in Redfern in December 1971. The inspection report noted that the property they were living in had been condemned after incurring blast damage from nearby construction and was barely habitable. It was noted that the 'home is well maintained under the circumstances and is well and tastefully furnished' (class cultural judgements as well as those of race were being exercised here). The children were deemed to be well cared for and the hygiene standards were high, notwithstanding the state of the premises. The report noted that D was in stable employment and had been 'in the same job since being discharged from the army'. The family was 'not known locally to police' and was willing to accept dormitory accommodation anywhere except in the areas of high concentrations of Aboriginal people 'in Mt Druitt or La Perouse'. A file note indicates the desire of the family to start a new life:

> The family is a reputable one. The have made honest and successful efforts to establish and maintain a high moral and emotional tone in the home. They have been plagued by relatives encroaching upon them and desire to be free of this type of environment (ST 2210 Box 14/1424).

The file notes do not make it clear whether the family retained contact with relatives. A house in Bradbury near Campbelltown in Sydney was eventually allocated to them. They rented from the Commission for four years from March 1975 and were considered good and reliable tenants. In 1979 they vacated the Commission house having purchased a dwelling in the area. This smooth transition from inner-city slum or reserve housing to home ownership was atypical. Most files demonstrate some evidence of conflict around community, culture and/or rental obligations.

Families and Conflict on Government Estates

The HFA programme gave suburban tenancies to many Aboriginal people who, because of competition with non-Indigenous applicants, would not have otherwise achieved this goal. Those who were fortunate enough to satisfy the Housing Commission gatekeepers and obtain tenancies were often subject to intrusive surveillance. Of the Indigenous tenants who had been accepted prior to HFA the chair of the Housing Commission, Purcell, stated, 'we have to be more intense with our attention to them' (Joint Committee 1967, p. 31). Even after the establishment of HFA, Commission officers consistently treated tenants as if they were in receipt of privileges. In return for state largesse they were expected to conform to social-engineering pressures. Some willingly severed ties with their communities and met Commission expectations. The great majority, however, endeavoured to sustain their links in some way, to sustain a way of life that often conflicted with the Commission's vision of respectable suburbia. Their actions, the behaviour of children and relatives, often resulted in conflict with neighbours and Commission officers. Housing Files contain letters of complaint, which were sent to the Commission, and copies of investigation reports that resulted. In what follows I will explore the sources of complaints about Indigenous tenants. These concerned the concentration of large groups of Aboriginal people together (whether authorised by the Commission or not), the associated rowdy public behaviour and the perceived misbehaviour of children.

Bringing the Mission to Town

Many Aboriginal people today who live in concentrated population groups in town housing experience stigma that is little different from that they experienced in out-of-town reserves. Aboriginal enclaves in country towns – West Dubbo,[12] Tolland in Wagga Wagga, the south side of Inverell are examples – and metropolitan suburban areas like Airds near Campbelltown, attract racist labels ('Vegemite valley') such that there is little chance of achieving the public policy aims of integration. The suburban dispersal practices that were favoured by the Commission in the early 1970s created loneliness and isolation. In situations of large group relocation, however, the 'salt and pepper' policies were often not followed, for example when several hundred Indigenous residents of Housing Commission dwellings in Surry Hills and Redfern, in inner Sydney, were moved to Airds, on the south-western periphery. Such a strategy fostered Indigenous solidarity, but made residents vulnerable to attacks of a more generalised racist character. Even those Aboriginal people who conformed and followed the strictures of the planners and bureaucrats suffered the slur associated with living in a 'black ghetto'.

GF who lived with his wife and children in a pocket of HFA housing in Kempsey illustrates this problem (ST 586 Box 14/1453). The F family, previously living on the Burnt Bridge reserve, was allocated town housing in the early seventies in an area in which 10 other Aboriginal households were accommodated. A letter signed by seven non-Indigenous neighbours in March 1973 stated:

> The language uttered by these people when in any form of anger or anxiety usually centres on a four letter word relative to copulation and is frequently used in conjunction with a slang word for a part of the female anatomy. Many of the neighbours, and indeed the Aboriginals themselves, have young children who ... should not be subjected to such experiences. The ab. children have been seen urinating from windows and even standing on the steps. I have personally seen all this and have also witness [sic] one boy of about eight years relieving bowel pressures under the house.

The letter went on to complain that sleep patterns were disturbed when their Aboriginal neighbours arrived home late at night in a drunken state.

> I am aware that it is the Minister for Housing's policy to try and assimilate these ab. people into the normal community. These people are not aware of the standards required for peaceful coexistence and in most cases disregard other people's property. When the head of the home at No2 [M] Street was confronted about his children running freely through my yard his reply was that his children can run through my yard if they

want to. Plants provided by the Housing Commission have been badly damaged.

An investigation undertaken by the Commission found that the complaints had some validity. The report in April 1973 found that the houses of the Indigenous families were too close together 'with only fifty yards from one cottage to the other'. It also observed that many of the families appeared to be innocent but were tarred with the same brush as those who were responsible for much of the disruption. The report found the condition of the F family house to be 'hardly satisfactory' and that there was 'a derelict vehicle at the rear of the grounds'. It went on to state:

> Within this particular area there are at present nine HFA cottages with another five bedroom dwelling under construction, as well as two Aboriginal families who have been housed under the ordinary programme. Keeping in mind the No. of Aboriginal families who are attracted by the presence of these families it appears that saturation point has been reached ... and should further allocations be made or HFA cottages built, it would not be in the best interests of the present assimilation programme.

The F family eventually negotiated a transfer to another location in the Kempsey area. The case indicates how many non-Indigenous tenants allocated blame on a generalised racist basis and not according to who was actually responsible.

Neighbourhood Conflicts and the Control of Children

Many of the neighbourhood conflicts involving Aboriginal people were based on the behaviour of children. When they moved to town housing young children encountered restrictions on their movement the like of which had not existed on reserves or in camps. Aboriginal people today who knew reserve life only as young people often recall their early experiences with great fondness. The poverty, hardship and petty intrusions of reserve life were less important to them than were the collective pleasures of childhood which were largely based on being able to move across large areas of land.

On reserves housing was not organised around strictly delineated private blocks. The Welfare Board had made efforts to encourage residents to cultivate gardens, to express 'civic pride' in preparation for assimilation. These were based on a notion of individual or nuclear family custodianship over small parcels of ground, something incompatible with communities based on extended families and with traditional cultural relationships to the land, and were usually unsuccessful. The case of PM, who lived on Purfleet reserve near Taree and applied for town housing in 1974, illustrates this point:

> The interior of the home is comfortably furnished and is maintained in a good condition. Although the yard is neat, Mr. [M's] attempts to est. gardens have not succeeded due to vandalism by other members of the community (ST 1987 Box 14/1453).

Aboriginal parents generally had more children than non-Indigenous people. Those who obtained tenancies with one or two children would very often go on to have several others. The houses that they had been allocated became too small to accommodate the growing numbers. The opportunities to transfer were, however, restricted. Most of the Housing Commission stock was made up of three-bedroom bungalows. There were limited numbers of larger dwellings of four bedrooms, but these were in great demand and were in any case not sufficient to house families of eight and nine children, and any additional family members. Not only did the Commission seek to build houses and communities around a nuclear family norm, but there was also very little flexibility for families with more than four children. When Aboriginal women, particularly those whose husbands were often away from home, moved into town housing away from the day-to-day support which was provided by extended family members, they often found it difficult to control large numbers of children.

The case of the B family of Broken Hill illustrates this well (ST 2179 Box 14/1424). AB and JB, who already had several children, applied for housing in 1971 and were assessed in the following terms:

> The care of children in gen. satis. espec. in view of the fact that there is no elec. connected and water has to be carried ... some three hundred

yards. Being of pt. Aboriginal extraction, this family's cult. standards would be n'less acceptable to any community.

They were offered town housing and by 1974 there were nine children under the age of eleven. AB was employed as a sheep shearer and his intermittent work made it difficult for the family to meet regular rental payments. He was frequently absent during shearing season. In May 1975 neighbours petitioned the Commission to remove the B family from the area. They referred to them as 'undescribable (sic) tenants because of the children's actions. Trespassing also taking things from neighbours yards, also using filthy language'. Later letters included reports of the children being violent towards non-Indigenous children, throwing stones through windows, breaking into houses, stealing pets and toys and defecating in public.

The Commission investigated the complaints and found them to be justified. They solicited a report from the Department of Youth and Community Services on the situation of the family that stated:

> One of the family's biggest problems is that Mr [B] has always been an absentee father, first as a shearer and now in his work for the Aboriginal community. He spends a good deal of his time in Sydney leaving his wife to cope with a family of nine children ... Mrs [B] is a very inadequate mother and housekeeper who shows only surface interest in her children and home. The children behave reasonably well when their father is at home but during his absences Mrs [B] has no control and she actively encourages their delinquent behaviour by hiding it from her husband ... She excuses all her shortcomings ... by taking the attitude that the entire community is racially prejudiced against her family.

Welfare accounts such as this provided an explanation of family problems, but they rarely served to assist tenants in their efforts to retain their houses. For the Housing Commission the social climate of the neighbourhood was the paramount concern. The family was evicted in December 1975.

Extended family members – neighbours' complaints

The presence of members of extended family in the household posed a challenge to the Housing Commission. Extended family relationships are central to Aboriginal culture and community and most tenants were unwilling to refuse hospitality to those relatives who came to visit.[13] For many Aboriginal people (as a consequence of the discrimination experienced at the hands of real-estate agents and landlords) the homes of relatives living in Commission houses were the only alternative to living on the streets or in squats. Those who took them in were in breach of rules that stated that only those listed in the tenancy agreement should reside in the dwelling. Officers frequently made notes about those who appeared to them to be living in houses while not registered on the tenancy list. Aboriginal people suffered constant surveillance and a good deal of harassment about their living arrangements.

In many cases neighbours complained about the noise and disruption and therefore drew the Commission's attention to the fact that relatives had arrived to live in the house. FD, a middle-aged widow with four older children, successfully applied for a house in the mid-seventies in the northern New South Wales town of Casino (ST 4397 Box 14/1455). A neighbour wrote in a letter to the Commission:

> I don't know how many people are supposed to be living there but some nights it sounds like the whole tribe is camped there. On several occasions there has been drugs mentioned by them ... For 6 months our sleep has been very disturbed by the constant yelling and the barking of dogs. Christmas night decided me to write you this letter, as all hell broke loose in there and the police were finally called ... The police came and took three of them away, later that night the fights broke out again. I can't understand why you can't keep all the darkies in one area and that way you would confine the misery to one area instead of spreading it all over town. We have even thought about selling our house, but decided this would get us nowhere as we would lose thousands of dollars while we have neighbours like these.

Many areas in which HFA tenants were located contained a mixture of public and private housing. The latter included those mainstream tenants who had moved from renting to purchasing their Commission dwellings. In addition to neighbourhood amenity, defence of property values was a major source of conflict between Indigenous and non-Indigenous people.

PD applied for a house in 1975 on behalf of himself, wife, baby daughter and 60-year-old father (ST 4529 Box 14/1456). They were living at the time in a household of 14 people, six adults and eight children, and were approved for town housing in Inverell. In the early stages of the tenancy they maintained the house to the satisfaction of the Commission but fell into rent arrears. They were the focus of neighbour complaints alleging frequent wild parties. A letter petition signed by 24 residents in December 1977 stated that 'In the last two weeks there have been five all night drunken parties with swearing, yelling, screaming and fighting all night and using the back yard as a toilet'. When one neighbour complained to the party-goers he was 'threatened with a smack in the mouth'. The petition stated 'there is a woman and three children living there ... who shouldn't be there'. A Commission officer investigating found that 'they do not arrange the parties but friends arrive in a drunken state and are very hard to move on'. The disruptions even drew a mention in the local newspaper, the *Inverell Times* (14 December 1977). By the middle of 1978 the rental arrears were such that the family was issued with a Notice to Quit the premises. It came to light that the listed tenants were no longer in occupation, that PD had left his sister in charge of the house while he travelled elsewhere to work as a tobacco picker, family in tow. This seasonal work meant that they were absent quite frequently for periods of six to eight weeks, during which time rental payments were not maintained, and many of the noisy parties and brawls occurred. The occupants of the house were evicted at the end of August 1978. This case demonstrates that Aboriginal people who survived on the irregular income of seasonal work found it difficult to meet the regular rental payments expected of tenants. The Housing Commission was geared to dealing with households with steady incomes.

The case also shows that the conventional idea of residency, with all the expectations this involved, did not fit with the culture and lifestyle of many Aboriginal people. Movement between city and bush, or one town and another, during which time houses were often left in the care of relatives, meant that Aboriginal people were not model tenants. Commission operational structures were built around the idea of the nuclear family, usually with a male breadwinner, who would occupy a dwelling constantly except for brief holiday periods. They did not easily accommodate the living and working arrangements of some Aboriginal tenants.

Falling Between the Cracks – Aboriginal People Denied Public Housing

Although much of this chapter and the next is concerned with the experiences of those who lived in Housing Commission dwellings, the Aboriginal housing files illustrate, often painfully, the plight of others who were unsuccessful, many of whom made multiple applications. Many of those who demonstrated such persistence were transient, frequently searching for the sort of stability that the ever-elusive Housing Commission dwelling would provide. Their inability to find adequate housing in circumstances of shortage clearly contributed to (but does not completely explain) their social marginalisation. A Commission tenancy might well have improved life chances. This section will present two case studies of families who fell between the cracks. The first family strove to break down institutional racism before the introduction of HFA, the second applied several times in the period after the introduction of the scheme.

The T Family[14]

LT and his wife J were exceptional in that they first applied to the Housing Commission in 1945, well before most Indigenous people were given any encouragement to seek public housing or were likely to make a claim for it. The tone of letters attached to L's original application indicates that he believed strongly in his right to assistance from the state and felt that he should be treated in the same way as any non-Aboriginal applicant. The file traces the movement of a family from the city back to the country after housing applications were unsuccessful.

In 1945 L, working as a labourer and living in cramped dilapidated circumstances in Waterloo, applied for accommodation for himself, his wife and seven children. The inspector's report of 30 May that year opened in a tone of incredulity: *These people are Aboriginals . . . I could not make any rec. other than bad* (quoted more extensively above). Oblivious to this judgement, and having apparently not received any notification of rejection, L sent a letter in February of the following year. In this he pleaded for housing and pointed out that his wife was expecting their tenth child (there is no explanation of the fate or whereabouts of the two not living with them).

As their circumstances worsened he wrote further letters in September and October of the same year seeking emergency accommodation. The second of these read:

> I have been compelled to send my wife and children to the country where they are living in a two room hut ... My wife and five children are sleeping in one bed in a single room and three boys are sleeping in a bed in the kitchen ... I have had an application for a home for two years but am still without. I have been forced to leave my job in Sydney through no accommodation but can get it back as soon as I get a home.

He went on to write that his family was living near Cowra in a humpy located some distance from a dam, their only water supply. Further applications were lodged in 1947 with a letter from L in that year written from the bush indicating his desire to move back to the city. Their application was placed in a ballot in 1950 at a time when this was a popular means of allocating housing. They were unsuccessful.

Nothing else appears on the file until 1959 when J applied from an address in Enmore where she was living with eight children. L had died in the intervening period. The inspection report of October of that year states 'This family were living at the Aboriginal mission home at Cowra. Except for two years they have lived there all their lives'. It went on to relate that J had brought her family to the city because there was no work for her elder daughters in Cowra. They were working in a chocolate factory in Redfern. The report commented on the overcrowding which they were experiencing but stated that J appeared to be a good housekeeper and looked after her children well. They were recommended for emergency accommodation. Nothing was offered to her, the family moved and the Commission was unable to track them down when, after some time, a place became available.

A further application was received in 1966. It was accompanied by a letter from Charles Perkins, the head of the Foundation for Aboriginal Affairs (an early advocacy body for Indigenous city dwellers), who claimed that J had been on the waiting list for ten years to no avail. The Commission responded by saying they had been unable to track down the applicant when a house had been allocated to her previously. In 1967 yet another application form was lodged, stating a Newtown address. The inspecting officer reported that J, now 59 years old, was living on her own. When he visited her, embittered by her past treatment, she had berated him and accused the Housing Commission of being racist. A bed-sit was allocated to her but she never took up the offer.

This file illustrates how the failure of the state to provide accommodation at a crucial point in the lives of L and J extinguished their hopes for a better life in the city and consigned them back to a humpy on the riverbank. This was a time of considerable prejudice. Their energetic claims were never likely to succeed because the state had not yet accepted that Aboriginal people had any right to live in cities alongside non-Indigenous citizens. This was reflected in the tone of the inspector's notes in response to the original application where he expressed his alarm that the family were resident in the city and his incredulity at their effrontery in applying for Housing Commission housing. Although there was a significant Aboriginal community in the inner city it appears that there was little public recognition of its presence until the late 1940s.

By the 1960s the Commission was much more responsive and sympathetic to J's claims. The inspection report appears less motivated by racist judgement and the language of the file notes reflect a shift from a modality of charity in the 1940s to one involving a limited notion of the rights of applicants 20 years later. In 1967, J's belligerence when confronted with the Commission officer clearly demonstrates her personal frustration that the social and material life improvements which her family had pursued in the 1940s, were denied to them by the gatekeepers of the Commission. Yet it may also represent a political obstreperousness based on feeling part of an emerging Aboriginal rights movement.

The Q Family[15]

The Q family left Walgett in Western New South Wales in early 1968 when work ran out in the drought-stricken area, and moved south to Warren where they applied for mainstream Housing Commission housing. The application form filled out by AQ lists herself, her husband D and their six children. They were living on the Beemunnell reserve when the inspector visited them in August and his report stated 'Applicant is Aboriginal, living conditions primitive. Shack filthy and strong stench, rubbish litters the yard'. Such references to primitivism recur frequently in Commission inspection reports on applicants, eliding a cultural judgement with a description of domestic circumstances. Living conditions were 'primitive' not 'squalid' or 'appalling'. The tension between sympathy and judgement, apparent in the Q file, is typical of the operation of the modernist state. The inspector deemed the applicants 'unfit' for Commission accommodation but noted that 'housing need definitely exists. I feel that intermediate type accommodation is required'. The Aboriginal housing files contain numerous other examples of similar notes referring to the need for transitional housing to promote phased assimilation for Aboriginal families.

The family next applied for HFA housing in March 1971. By this time D was 39, A 33 and they had eight children. As was common at the time, they had obtained furniture on hire purchase. Notwithstanding this the inspector reported 'wife has been advised to lift their standards. Genuine housing need exist'. The decision was to defer allocation of housing until improvements in standard of domestic housekeeping were manifested, but no follow-up inspections appear to have occurred.

A further application was lodged in 1975 from Walgett. The inspector here recommended in November of that year that a decision on the application be deferred while the applicants were counselled on home making and child-rearing skills. In February 1976 the Gilgandra office received an application that listed only A and the eight children. The Commission officer here determined that a housing need existed as the family was living in a situation of gross overcrowding. Applicants were to be admitted subject to a welfare report. Before this process could be carried through the family moved to the city to live in Redfern and the parents had been reunited.

They applied for HFA housing again in April of 1977 and only six children were listed as being resident. The eldest boy was being held in the remand centre pending charges for car theft and the second son was completing his schooling in Walgett. D was unemployed and 'he came in during the visit. He was obviously under the influence of alcohol'. Observations about sobriety and drunkenness appear frequently in the HFA files although hardly ever in the mainstream files. The Commission officer reported that he asked A if she would accept counselling from another government employee on housekeeping. She refused and said she would do it alone. There is clear evidence running through the file of a strong resistance to assimilationist pressures. Aboriginal women were usually at the coalface here. They yearned for better living conditions in which to bring up their children but were too proud to accept the demeaning tutelage and direction of social workers and other 'experts'.

The next application for housing was one year later in March 1978. The form indicated that the family sought to be housed in the Mt Druitt region, Western Sydney, rather than in the inner city. Appended to this application was a letter from an administrator of the Rachel Foster Hospital to the Housing Commission. This indicated that A had been an in-patient there several times since March 1977, the latest time for more than one month. The letter stated that during these periods the family suffered severe hardships. A daughter, 14, had run away from home and appeared before a children's court. Two sons aged 12 and 13 had also run away from home and were only located when one of them was involved in a car accident in a stolen car. Those in the family house in Redfern were living in overcrowded conditions with poor hygiene. The furniture had been bought at a charity shop. The oven was not working and only two hot plates were connected. The letter reported that a consequence of this was that the children were malnourished. D had obtained employment with the New South Wales Railways. The letter reported that he had an irregular pattern of attendance at work, but that this was improving.

By the time a Commission inspection was organised the Q family had been evicted from the house in Caroline Street and, in quick succession, from a house in Newtown. D was living in the Aboriginal hostel in Chippendale, adjacent to the city with two children and A in another form of temporary accommodation in Arncliffe in the city's south. Daughter J had returned to Walgett where she was facing breaking and entering charges. In spite of the dire circumstances and the clear welfare need the family was refused HFA housing. They were informed that they had to establish themselves in private rental and show themselves to be worthy before they could be considered for a Commission place. Following this determination there were letters from the Department of Youth and Community Services and from the New South Wales Minister for Mines and Energy, Pat Hills, whose electorate covered the Redfern/Chippendale area, pleading with the

Housing Minister on behalf of the family. These were to no avail. Ron Mulock, the minister, wrote back saying his officers would arrange private housing for the family and reassess them at a later stage.

In 1979, A applied for emergency accommodation. She was living at the time in a Salvation Army hostel at La Perouse and had recently left her husband at the house they were renting in Granville 'because of his drunkenness and cruelty'. Four of the younger children were with her at the hostel and the two older sons remained with D in Granville. The file at this point contains a memo of a phone conversation between the Housing Commission officer and the head of the hostel in which the latter stated that A had no control over her children and that they would be 'better off in state care'.

Showing remarkable persistence in the face of adversity, A next applied for housing in July 1980. She was living in Tempe with five children and her 19-year-old son who had a job. There were more letters from the Department of Youth and Community Services requesting favourable consideration. The Commission officer who inspected wrote that he suspected they had made an effort to clean up prior to his arrival but that 'The walls were marked and the carpet stained. There was the smell of cat urine on the floor'. He recommended a deferral of the decision.

The final entry in the file was a memo dated November 1980. It reported that the Commission officer called without an appointment at the Tempe flat and that the caretaker and neighbours reported that the occupants had done a 'moonlight flit' leaving rental arrears and the dwelling in an appalling state. They alleged that 14 people had been in occupation, that the children were uncontrollable, that rubbish was dumped everywhere and that the police had been called frequently because of drunken parties. On inspection they found that 'old furniture and rubbish was piled high and that all front windows had been smashed'.

How to understand the descending fortunes of the Q family? Clearly improved housing would not have been a panacea. Yet there is little doubt that poor, overcrowded accommodation contributed to the cycle of decline. The one older child who showed promise in education remained in the bush while other family members moved to the city. In HFA files, inspection reports frequently observed that the cramped domestic circumstances made it practically impossible for children to study in quiet conditions.

Yet what is suggested in the Q file, as with so many others like it, is that the quest for improved housing had a gender dimension. It was women who very often initiated the applications for Commission housing yet it was they who usually bore the brunt of the moral judgements that accompanied their rejection. AQ continued to invite the gaze of the state in a desperate quest for material improvement. This process in itself must have seemed perilous. The judgements extended beyond the sphere of domestic cleanliness and housekeeping to observations about parenting and the circumstances of the children. The threat of the 'welfare' removing children from the family might have deterred many others from making applications. The systematic removal of Aboriginal children from their parents had ceased by the 1970s when administrators became more careful about acting on the racist judgements which had informed child welfare practice for so long. But many Aboriginal parents were unaware of this, continued to mistrust the state and to be haunted by the practices of the past.

In the Q file and in many others, marital conflict appears central. Often the Commission would find out about domestic violence through the representations of neighbours or community or state organisations. In many cases inspecting officers would draw inferences (whether accurate or inaccurate) from what they observed on visiting the family. Frequently, where domestic violence triggered the application for housing or contributed to the breakdown of families that had taken up a tenancy, alcohol was mentioned as being involved. As is generally the case, the documents revealed that Aboriginal women usually made efforts to conceal the violent circumstances they faced, particularly to white administrators, up to the point of family breakdown. The solidarity of Aboriginal people across gender lines has often confounded the efforts of the women's movement to confront such violence (Burgmann 1982).

The story of the Q family is not unusual. Their housing file tells a story of a 12-year period, depicting a journey from bush to city and of social trauma occasioned by poverty, alcohol, and separation. Other Aboriginal people in the mid- to-late twentieth century commonly confronted such problems. The closure of the AWB and the allocation of its functions to various mainstream government departments did little to ameliorate their plight and indeed might have made it worse by separating the functions of housing and social welfare. The principled rhetoric about equality and inclusion for

Aboriginals mouthed by those who sponsored the reforms of the late 1960s was not achieved by the administrative structures they put in place.

Conclusion

Despite the state's formal recognition from 1969 that Aboriginal people had the right to live *as Aboriginal people* in cities and towns, the day-to-day administration of housing policy was informed more by the ideology assimilation than by liberal notions of integration. The HFA programme provided the opportunity for them to move into suburban housing as never before. Although demand outstripped supply, many of those who had lived in substandard housing could now enjoy living conditions previously unavailable to them. Nevertheless the HFA was not a programme based on pluralistic tolerance of Indigenous culture. Aboriginal applicants were measured against the same yardsticks as were applied to mainstream applicants. They had to demonstrate that they were both keen to, and capable of, making the transition to a suburban lifestyle, one of solid nuclear family values: modesty, privacy, strictly delineated gender roles, hard work, cleanliness and moral rectitude. Many of these standards were alien to Aboriginal people. They resisted the pressures and expectations placed on them. The HFA files show that one of the central assumptions of the early town planning movement–that people are socially and morally transformed if they are given a better environment in which to live–is incorrect. Most Aboriginal people strove to retain their culture and links to community and resisted the social-engineering pressures that were placed on them. Some sought to escape and to sever links with communities but most sought to accommodate their social and cultural baggage.

The process of bringing large numbers of Aboriginal people under the umbrella of the Housing Commission was achieved when policy makers made the decision in the late 1960s to move from Aboriginal-specific to mainstream service provision. This was based on progressivist liberal thinking, namely that Indigenous people should enjoy the same rights and responsibilities as other citizens. However this also meant that the state dealt with Aboriginality through discrete bureaucratic categories–housing, health, welfare etc. The practices and policy imperatives associated with each bureaucracy were specific to the areas that they covered and paid little attention to the agendas of those dealing in the other areas. The structures and policies of the Housing Commission, for example, did not recognise the overlaps of health, housing and welfare. Welfare considerations were of marginal concern to those allocating housing. It was rare for Aboriginal people to be allocated housing on compassionate grounds. Nor was the Housing Commission equipped or designed to deal with family problems: domestic violence, children who were upsetting neighbours and so on. The standard response was to seek to restore neighbourhood order, even if this meant evicting unruly tenants. Neither the paternalistic racism of the AWB, nor the impersonal modernist regime of the Housing Commission was congenial to Aboriginal people and their ways of life. In the new mainstream bureaucratic regimes, they were addressed as individual families and citizens. These categories did not adequately incorporate their histories, cultures and aspirations.

It is important not to treat the conflict that has been explored in this chapter only in racial terms. The structures of urban development and social control were generated by struggles dating back to the turn of the century to which Aboriginal people were marginal. The town planning movement was formulating its ideas about the ideal form of the city in a period in which it was taken for granted that Aboriginal people were appropriately located outside of urban spaces. Public housing programmes were largely designed to produce declasse suburban citizens – to provide those worthy and respectable members of the inner-city working class a place in which they could live decent lives away from the slums, overcrowding and dilapidation of the inner city. The Housing Commission was principally an agency which provided a start for the deserving poor but it operated on the basis that families had not only to establish need but also moral worthiness. The racist character of Housing Commission practices and policies was a contingent and not a primary condition of its operation. While racism certainly informed the views and actions of Housing Commission officers – they frequently made stereotypical assessments of Aboriginal applicants and tenants – in many respects the regulation of class and gender was much more important.

Chapter 5

Unsettling Narratives

The previous three chapters showed how Aboriginal people resisted the central assumption of the narrative of assimilation: that by living alongside non-Indigenous people in towns and cities, they would jettison their communal/cultural bonds and become absorbed into a suburban monoculture. This chapter explores a series of counter narratives. These are the life histories of four people who were able to sustain and reconstruct their Aboriginal identities in the face of pressures to assimilate in the conservative social climate that prevailed in post-war Australia.

Oral History Method and Aboriginality

To this point we have looked at source materials that represent Aboriginality mostly in snapshot. Indigenous people generally appear only fleetingly in archives and other public documents. Where their actions are viewed only through the filter of official representations, they show up as passive victims or as reacting impulsively to the exercise of power. They dart in and out of the official/ colonial field-of-vision, appearing only where they pose problems to authorities and disappearing when those problems subside. Most such source material permits only synchronic analysis, meaning it is often particularly difficult to fully comprehend particular actions, be they resistant or compliant. By contrast, the case studies presented below are based on interviews with Aboriginal people who moved to the city in the post-war years and became tenants of the Housing Commission.

In his important book *The Voice of the Past* British historian Paul Thompson described oral history as an egalitarian alternative to conventional disciplinary research practice (Thompson 1978). He argued that historians should move beyond the inert sources of the archives and where possible speak to those who witnessed and/or participated in the historical processes and events under scrutiny. Its proponents view oral history as democratic, as providing a voice to those who have no other capacity to shape the public representation of the past. Their stories can shape the social histories that provide alternatives to conventional 'great men' accounts of the past.

Oral history has had considerable appeal to those working in Aboriginal studies. Several authors have compiled collections of transcribed oral narratives (Tatz and McConnochie 1975; Gilbert 1977; Rintoul 1993). Others have written practical oral history guidelines for Aboriginal researchers (Taylor 1992). Those who advocate undertaking oral research amongst Indigenous people point to the importance of oral narratives in traditional cultures, and to the fact that their low levels of literacy have excluded them from producing their own written historical accounts. The inclusion of life histories based on oral narratives allows us to consider how particular individuals responded to changes in social structure over a relatively long period and how their actions reinforced or disrupted prevailing practices and institutional arrangements.

On the other hand oral history method has been cogently criticised for its empiricist tendencies. The authors of *Making Histories* suggest that the ideas of Thompson 'rest on arguments about alternative content and transformative practice on the nature of the historical source itself' (Popular Memory Group, Centre for Contemporary Cultural Studies 1982, p. 223). Oral historians generally pay little attention to the subjective, cultural and political processes involved both in recalling/speaking of the past and in writing accounts based on those recollections. Both oral testimony and the resultant written history are culturally encoded. Interviewees do not simply communicate facts. They also draw on 'all the symbolic and linguistic features through which meaning is conveyed' to tell their stories (p. 225). The process of remembering and speaking of the past is, like all history writing, shaped by contemporary concerns and social processes (including collective/communal influences). Biographical narratives are often teleological. They throw into sharp relief those events and aspects of life which stand in contrast to or appear to have determined contemporary social situations.

In evaluating oral history methods for the purposes of studying Indigenous cultures anthropologists have offered similar criticisms (Morris 1995; Barwick 1981). Morris argues that much oral history operates around humanist assumptions; that it runs the risk of reducing historical narrative to the 'actions of historical persons' (p. 84) and of not recognising that oral testimony 'is embedded in culturally specific forms or sociality and social practice' (p. 90). Oral history research amongst those from other cultures necessarily involves a process of translation that those working only in an empiricist vein often fail to recognise. Those working with Indigenous Australians should be cognisant of the importance of orality in traditional culture and how the conventions of oral transmission might shape the biographical interview. Barwick claims that while the oral historian might interpret what s/he hears from an Aboriginal person as an individual tale, it is often predominantly about family rather than self. Morris observes that traditional narratives were organised around references to places, to significant and sacred sites, rather than on a linear temporal basis. Where things happened was more important than when. Goodall makes a similar point when discussing dreaming stories (Goodall 1996, pp. 2–6). She also argues, *contra* functionalist anthropology, that these traditional narratives are able to incorporate recent (ie post-invasion) events even though they are organised spatially and in terms that historians view as mythological rather than historical.

There is no doubt that traditional narrative and genealogical structures exert considerable influence on the stories of those who live in longstanding communities in remote areas on or close to their traditional land. However, for Indigenous people who live in cities the significance of such forms is diminished. Their personal narratives are overlaid with the larger public stories, collective and individual, and framed by contemporary social relations. Although each of my interview subjects had a strong sense of Aboriginal identity, as urban dwellers they are more detached than were their forebears from home country and culture. For two of them extended family continued to be important, although relationships to kin were very different to traditional ones. Contemporary culture and social relations have assumed increasing significance. It is important, therefore, not to reify and essentialise the differences between Aboriginal and non-Aboriginal people, and to strive to translate Indigenous memory into a form intelligible to non-Indigenous people.

To understand why and how Indigenous people tell their stories to researchers it is necessary to move beyond archetypal oral forms to explore contemporary influences. On top of the generic narrative forms circulating in popular culture there are also those which relate specifically to Indigenous experiences. For example, in recent years there have been numerous Aboriginal biographies appearing in the media. The findings of the Royal Commission into Aboriginal Deaths in Custody and the Human Rights and Equal Opportunity Commission's enquiry into the Stolen Generations referred to a number of life histories, many of which were publicised in newspapers. These have established the genre of welfare 'case histories' in the public sphere and have almost certainly helped to give Aboriginal people the confidence to speak of aspects of their lives where in the past they would have been reticent. This is true of my four interviewees, who have been involved in Aboriginal community organisations and are conscious of contemporary black-white politics. They have become aware that there is a general public interest and perhaps more sympathy than existed in the past.

In addition, the flowering of Aboriginal autobiography, particularly among women, has provided another possible source of influence (Morgan 1987; Langford 1988; Sykes 1997). Sabbioni argues that these works emerge from the *yarning* cultures of Aboriginal communities (Sabbioni 1996). This may well be so. However, the effect of these publications on Indigenous people in all settings must be to enhance a sense that biographical narratives are important even (and perhaps particularly) where they describe experiences of poverty and discrimination, rather than prominent public achievements. My interviewees understood why I considered their experiences to be significant. They were not puzzled as to why I wished to interview them.

In what follows I have constructed the life history narratives of Millicent, Hilary, Keith and Joyce from the transcripts of the interviews I conducted with them. I do not, however, confine myself to simply telling the stories. I also read *through* them to identify the underlying social structural forces that shaped life courses. Interviewees may well narrate large changes in their lives as the product of individual choice, but in our reading of their words we should seek to uncover the social dimensions of such choices, to develop a sociological understanding of the narratives. Interviewees (including the four here) are often keenly aware of these sociological dimensions.

While taking the content and empirical reference points of interviewees' narratives seriously, I am not strictly or centrally concerned with measuring the veracity of their recollections. There may well be factual inaccuracies in what I have been told because memory is notoriously unreliable. Neither am I interested in events *per se*, but rather in the structures behind those events, which can only be understood in abstract terms. It is important to move beyond common sense or individualistic rationale for actions, and to seek to uncover the forces that impel these things.

Millicent

Millicent[1] was born in Cowra in rural New South Wales in 1943. When she was three her family moved to Sydney because her father refused to live on a government reserve. They became part of a nascent Aboriginal community in the poor inner suburbs of Sydney. Along with many other Aboriginal people, Millicent's family rented privately in Alexandria. Their household was a destination for relatives who came down from the country. Millicent described the process of chain migration:

> *Our* house ... was a central point for my mother's family who came to the city to go to hospitals, to see doctors, to get glasses or false teeth, to go to second-hand shops, to get Xmas presents. We always had this steady stream of people coming.

Millicent's parents adapted to the influx of relatives with a cheerfulness and resourcefulness that was typical of Aboriginal inner-city households at the time:

> My mother was very good at making places for people to sleep. My father was a jack of all trades. So a place that was basically a two- or three-bedroom place was turned into a five-bedroom place.

The accommodation was basic and lacked amenities. The house had a small kitchen with a laundry/bathroom in a corrugated-iron lean-to room at the back, typical of poor inner-city housing at the time. Millicent recalls that her family got on well with their white working-class as well as their Aboriginal neighbours. Her father did not drink, was in regular employment and the family were well regarded by those around them. They were on speaking terms with the non-Indigenous people in their street but never socialised with them. In many ways, Millicent's family exemplified the industrious, resourceful, respectable and mutually supportive values characteristic of the traditional proletarian urban village.

One of the chief reasons that her parents gave for moving to Sydney was to improve their children's life chances through education. Millicent, however, left school at 15, barely literate. Her recollections of schooling speak eloquently and poignantly of the ambiguities of urban Aboriginal identity:

> I always felt that I was expected to be the same as everybody else. There was never any conversation between teachers and Aboriginal students regarding the future. So there wasn't that relationship built between Aboriginal students and teachers. But you were always aware, without analysing it yourself, that you weren't really expected to produce the goods because they being non-aboriginal teachers didn't expect you to.

At one level her Aboriginality was barely acknowledged – there was certainly no recognition of her specific needs in the 1950s. But tacitly teachers saw her Indigenous background as indicating that she would inevitably fail. I discussed earlier the double standard that operated in the administration of housing. As we saw in the previous chapter, the formal public acceptance of Aboriginal people as tenants of the Housing Commission stood in contrast to the racist assumptions which informed the day-to-day workings of the Commission. Clearly similar processes also operated in education.

Her experience of education left Millicent with a sense of uncertainty about her own identity. Along with many other urban Indigenous people in the middle of the twentieth century, she was unclear about exactly where she fitted in. Most public representations – including those that circulated through school curriculum – described Indigenous culture in traditional terms:

> There was a lot of confusion because you know that what they're talking about wasn't the way you live. They're calling them Aborigines ... You grew to know that there was something wrong ... When I was going to school there was very little stuff on New South Wales Aborigines. The majority of stuff was on tribal. So there was never any qualification about these people here.

By implication, to live in a town or city was to compromise your Aboriginality. Your Indigenous side was simply a diminishing residue, a throwback to a less advanced phase of life.

In the face of these pressures, Aboriginal people were building solidarities and sub cultures in a new place. Most did not become involved in what were seen as white organisations and did not want to abandon their cultural and community ties. Millicent recalls, for example, that there was little involvement by Indigenous parents in school affairs. Those who went along to parents' and citizens' meetings were regarded 'as a big mouth or very assimilated'. Millicent recalls that most parents struggled to reinforce their children's Indigenous identities:

> M: So the parents hear their kids coming back from school and saying all sorts of things and they're thinking 'Oh assimilation, you know' some white ways are beginning to creep in here. To give ...
>
> Q: a shot of the old ways?
>
> M: No, because you're talking about New South Wales Aborigines here. To recharge them as Aborigines. Let me give you an analogy. It's a bit like when a white Australian goes overseas. He is more of an Australian than when he lives here. We as Aboriginal people in New South Wales don't get this type of recognition even from traditional people. We here are constantly reminding ourselves that we are Aborigines.

Millicent describes Aboriginality as something which has to be constantly nurtured and reinforced, something which is tenuous and under threat as a result of living in the city and which can be made solid again by visiting home country and community. She is aware that this is not about reclaiming the old ways.[2] It is about keeping the homogenising forces of modernity at bay. Millicent observed that most people saw the bush rather than Sydney as home:

> All the families who lived in Redfern etc did not belong there, they were migrants to Sydney. It's like if I have my kids in Crown St hospital Surry Hills, they don't belong there. They're Waradjuri *people*; they belong where I came from.

Her mother regularly took the children back to her people in the state's south-west. She would simply announce that they were going home for two days, but they would often stay away for two weeks or more at a time. This disrupted Millicent's education.

> In a lot of times the need overwhelmed the logic; the need to restrengthen their Aboriginality, their spirituality. In order to live here [in the city] and remain an Aborigine you have to go back and recharge your battery.

Later Millicent took her own children back home to encourage them to re-engage with their roots. She argues that Aboriginal people are very keen for their children to receive a good education, 'but not at the expense of their Aboriginality'.

Millicent got married at 18 to an Aboriginal man from the New South Wales north coast. They had three children and when the youngest was six months old, Millicent applied for a Housing for Aborigines (HFA) house. She remembers a Commission officer coming to inspect her parents' house where she was still living:

> My mother was ... always white-washing the cooking area. She went under tremendous stress when the housing department came out to look at the house ... all the people who were living in our house had to leave. You know the brothers their wives and the kids. If the [Housing Commission] person wanted to know if there were lots of people living there he only had to go to the people next door ... I think

> one of the questions was how many people are living there. I remember my sister saying 'What, did they ask that too? Why didn't they come and have a look at the fridge, you know.' You were given the third degree. As far as my mother was concerned I guess she might have thought that if the officer saw there were too many people living in this house then our house will become like that. 'Have you used an electric stove?' was asked. This was a new process ... The idea was assimilation and the Housing Commission would not want to be putting Aboriginal people next to non Aboriginal people if they're gonna have a million people coming to the house, if they can't cook on electric stove and were going to cook outside.

Millicent and her husband were offered an HFA home in Blackett, a part of Mt Druitt in western Sydney. She liked the house but the setting was very different from those she knew – the bush and the inner city – and it was far removed from the networks of support. Nevertheless they accepted the offer of housing believing there was little alternative for a young family at the time.

In her early period of living in the western suburbs, Millicent regularly trekked back into the centre in spite of the inadequacies of the public transport system ('it was a day exercise to commute back there to see people'). In the early days it was rare for Millicent's relatives, other than her parents, to travel out to visit her from the inner city or from Cowra:

> My mum would come out when she was in Sydney. But it's a bit like the family in the country, they're there and they're waiting. It's a bit like you've got into a boat and you've rowed out to sea and the shore can't come to you, you've got to come to the shore.

For people in Millicent's situation who had moved out from the inner city, the urban village and the home town were the centres of gravity until a significant Aboriginal presence was established in the outer suburbs. Perhaps the reluctance of these friends and relatives to visit was based on a feeling that they would be travelling to a territory, middle-class suburbia, where they would be out of place, where (at the time) few Aboriginal people were located.

Millicent felt alienated and displaced. She feared those around her would not accept her. She saw them as 'very middle classy' even though they were in rented Housing Commission dwellings, and although she was on polite greeting terms with neighbours, Millicent felt exposed ('more visible') than she ever had in the past. Her immediate neighbours, however, were white and were:

> looked down on by others in the street. Her husband would come home late and they would fight in the street. They did all the things that Aborigines were meant to do you know [laughs].

It was a few years before Millicent met other Aboriginal families living in the area.

She had difficulties coping with the social expectations that were placed on her as a Commission tenant, for example, how to use and tend to the space in and around her house. As a child in Alexandria she had 'played a lot out the front' of the house. The Blackett area, like most suburban estates, lacked this street culture. She was not happy that her children were confined to the quarter-acre block. At first they were not aware that they were expected to keep their garden trimmed:

> About three weeks after I moved in the lawn was very high and we didn't know anybody and we didn't have basically any money ... We didn't even think that having a long lawn was going to be a problem ... My biggest thing was to get a lawn mower. In those days you were told it was important to keep the outside of the house neat. I was threatened with eviction on two occasions because my lawn wasn't cut.

The local environment presented Millicent with difficulties that she had not encountered in the inner city. There were no shops in the vicinity. If she ran out of bread or milk she had to rely on her daughter to take care of the younger children while she undertook the half-hour walk to and from the nearest shops at Mt Druitt. At first she found it hard to navigate her way around the tangle of suburban streets which were designed in meandering Radburn fashion, rather than as a grid. She bought a second-hand pram and got into the habit of writing down the names of streets so that she could find her way home.

Soon after moving to the western suburbs Millicent's personal circumstances changed dramatically. Her husband had been unable to find work in the area. This placed stress on the relationship and her marriage ended. In addition, her parents moved from the city to Wellington in the central west of New South Wales. Although they came to stay with her often, they were less available to support her than was the case when they lived in Alexandria. This was a period of isolation and poverty. She eventually remarried but lived much of the late 1970s as a struggling single mother.

Her poverty meant that she was frequently in conflict with the Housing Commission:

> Aborigines in Mt.Druitt always had financial problems and if you had three children then, you certainly did not have the resources ... If the rent collector came to the door and you didn't have the money, you'd give them a sob story.

In spite of this Millicent made rental payment her highest priority. She recalls her mother telling her that 'you can always find a feed but you can't always get a roof over your head'. Like many Aboriginal tenants she got into rental arrears but not so deeply that she could not pull herself out. The door-to-door rent collection – a practice which was discontinued in the eighties – could be a demeaning and confronting experience:

> I had rent collectors who came to my place who wanted to come in every time and go through every bedroom. On one occasion started to look in my cupboards ... One guy ... came, and I had just washed the floor and the floor was all wet and I was sitting out on the steps. He wanted to go inside to talk to me and I said 'Look I've just washed the floor' and he proceeded to walk into my house and I decided that day that I would never pay my rent to the rent collector. I went down to the housing department and paid it.

There were also hazards for women alone in their houses. Millicent remembers hearing from other women who were Housing Commission tenants that rent collectors would seek sexual favours in return for waiving rental payments. Even when she paid her rent in the Housing Commission office Millicent was not spared humiliation:

> If you turned up [there] and you were behind in your rent you were … humiliated. The thing I dreaded more than anything was going to the [Housing Commission] to pay my rent. I used to worry about, have I worked it out properly. And seeing my rent collector down there because he would sing out 'Have you got all your rent today?' [stern tone] you know. And it used to get packed [with people] … it's humiliation … I remember going to see the supervisor of the [Housing Commission] regarding some problems that I had regarding the attitude of my rent collector. And this was a radical thing back then. I was told that I could not see the supervisor.

This experience of humiliation was probably common for Indigenous tenants but it is likely few were sufficiently assertive to complain as Millicent had. There was little difference between the treatment meted out by Commission officers and the paternalistic racism Aboriginal people had experienced at the hands of the AWB.

Millicent eventually found work in the city and was forced to spend long hours commuting. Her mother came to stay and help out with the children. This brought her into conflict with the Housing Commission:

> One of the things that we were told was that you could not have your family there. It was for you and your [immediate] family. And my parents came and my father wasn't well and they stayed for a couple of weeks and this Housing Commission guy came at eight o'clock at night and he said to me 'If these people are not gone, then you'll end up getting an eviction notice' and I was in tears. I was so upset …

It is ironic that while the Housing Commission was seeking to cultivate a suburban idyll based on delineating public and private space, and on confining personal matters to the latter, its staff encroached upon the privacy of Aboriginal tenants in such a cavalier fashion.

Like many of those who moved away from their people to the 'salt and pepper' isolation of the suburbs, Millicent developed a sense of being constantly watched by neighbours. She felt they expected her to lapse into the disruptive, anti-social habits of fringe dwellers. Ruby Langford wrote about experiencing a similar feeling at the Green Valley estate in south-west Sydney:

> But it got that way after a while that I was dying to see another black face like mine, someone to pass the time of day and yarn with, and if some relatives showed up for an occasional visit, when you went out to welcome them you could see your neighbours' curtains move and many eyes upon you. After a while I felt guilty about having visitors. I wondered who'd be dobbing me in to the Commission if the visitors stayed overnight (Langford 1988, p. 176).

Whether surveillance was real or imagined, what is significant is that Aboriginal tenants believed they were being watched.

In response to the overwhelming sense of alienation and loss of cultural anchorage, Millicent would occasionally take her children from school and travel back to Cowra in order, 'to restrengthen their Aboriginality, their spirituality'. In his classic study of metropolitan culture, Jonathon Raban argued that in contemporary urban life we can lose a sense of grounding in community and tradition. At this point the city begins to go 'soft' on us leading us to return to familiar places and people in order to reconfirm our identities, to counter the anomic state into which the city constantly draws us (Raban 1975). We attempt to reclaim what Tonnies called *gemeinschaft* to counter the impersonal and instrumental relations of modernity (Tonnies 1988). Millicent's return to home country was not only about bolstering Aboriginal identity. It was also part of a wider social response to urban modernism and alienation.

Millicent was scarred by her experiences with the Housing Commission. Like many others who were subject to the social engineering processes of public bureaucracies, she strove for independence. When she accumulated enough money to buy a house of her own she did so enthusiastically and escaped the clutches of the Commission that treated her at best with condescension and paternalism, at worst with racist harassment. She remained in the western suburbs but moved from Mt Druitt in the early 1980s. The area, always one of the poorest in the state, later became a major centre of Aboriginal population:

> Mt Druitt had a terrible stigma attached to it. You'd say 'I'm from Blackett.' and people'd say 'Oh where's Blackett?' and you'd say 'It's in Mt Druitt.' 'Oh.' [knowingly] If you were housed in Mt Druitt you were basically a misfit.

Millicent felt the social stigma that was associated with life in Mt Druitt. Home ownership, therefore, not only provided her with an opportunity to escape the racism of the Housing Commission but also to pursue social mobility in a more general sense.

Hilary

Hilary was born in Dubbo, a small country town in western New South Wales in 1955, one of 11 children. There was a rural downturn in the mid 1960s and when her father could no longer find work as a sheep-shearer, the family moved to Sydney. When they first arrived they were accommodated temporarily in the central Sydney headquarters of the Foundation for Aboriginal Affairs that supported Aboriginal families relocating to the city. Hilary recalls being awe struck by Sydney: the vastness of Central Station, the crowds, the lights and the traffic she could see from her room. All this was taken in from behind a pane of glass because she was told that she was too young to go out into the streets and had to remain in the building. The confinements associated with city life formed a recurring theme in Hilary's narrative of childhood.

From the city they moved to stay briefly with relatives at Warragamba Dam, on the rural outskirts of Sydney, where Hilary attended school. That was like being removed to the country again:

> No regular transport, no big shopping centres. And Warragamba was a tourist venue. So we used to go up to the dam wall and play up there ... And from there we moved to our own place at Silverdale ... It was private property that was rented out to Mum and Dad. By this time Dad was working I think. But it was really below standard housing. There was no water connected. Only one room had electricity. That

room became the kitchen, and no stove. Because I can remember Mum and Dad buying the electric saucepans and electric frying pans.

There were no other Aboriginal children in the area.

After Silverdale, the family lived in a number of 'sub-standard' dwellings on farms on the western fringe of Sydney. Although she was conscious that they were living in poverty, Hilary recalls this period as a happy one where she experienced a freedom of movement which was later to be denied to her ('it was all a new adventure'). At Mulgoa they lived in improvised housing which was supplied to farm workers:

We used to go and milk the cows and clean out the pig sties. Like all fun, you know. Well for me it was. And we used to get free milk, and Mum used to make butter from the milk. And if a pig was killed, we used to get some of the pig. Or Dad used to kill a pig himself, but there was no sewerage and overcrowded you know, because there were only three bedrooms.

One house had no electricity, only an old wood stove.

Hilary only attended school on an intermittent basis at this time because she was required to help out at home. Two babies were born after the family moved to Sydney and as is customary in Aboriginal families, she often had to miss school in order to help her mother to tend her younger siblings when they were sick. This peripatetic childhood disrupted Hilary's education. She changed schools frequently and found it hard to achieve academic success.

Her family experienced the most cramped circumstances of all while living in a house in Wallacia:

There was only one proper bedroom. And so Mum and Dad made up a room in the lounge room, with a big fireplace for us. And all the kids were stamped into this one bedroom. And where we were didn't have a bathroom or toilet, so it was communal bathroom and stuff. Again it didn't worry me, because we lived right behind the river.

It was only later, when she had her own child, that Hilary appreciated the pressure her mother must have been under at this time with so many to look after.

While at Wallacia Hilary's parents applied for Housing Commission housing. Hilary recalls her mother sending telegrams to the minister. She took this action when her youngest child was a baby, in 1969, just as the HFA scheme was established. There were frantic preparations for the arrival of the Housing Commission inspector:

> I can remember Mum making us all clean up ... She said 'This gubba [white man] from the Housing Commission is coming, get the place cleaned up. They're going to come out and they might give us a home'.

Hilary recalls that her mother had always been meticulous about housework:

> She said 'No matter what type of housing you live in, always keep it clean'. So even though we lived in sub-standard housing, I can always smell this very strong disinfectant, that Mum used to buy ... called 'Sandpick', and I used to hate the smell of it. But whenever the place was mopped out, it was mopped out with this stuff ... [this attitude came from] Mum's own experiences living on a mission, down in Cumaragunja in Victoria where the manager could come in at any time and do spot checks on your house on your premises.

On the day assigned for the Commission inspection the children help to clean up and were then told to make themselves scarce, 'So we just took off down the river'. In an earlier era Aboriginal children had run from welfare officials in fear that they would be taken from their parents, now they ran from Housing Commission inspectors so that the image of domestic harmony would not be compromised by the presence of too many of them. The strategy worked because, as Hilary recalls, very soon after the inspection they were moving into a Commission dwelling in Mt Druitt.

Hilary recalls that they were among the first Aboriginal families housed in Mt Druitt under HFA. They were allocated a four-bedroom house and seven children were still living at home. In her early years in Mt Druitt she yearned for the lifestyle she had experienced while living on farms on the urban fringe:

> I hated being there too, because we were trapped there. Because all the other places we lived at, we had free rein. We could just wander off, we could go to the river at any time ... The nearest river was probably 10 to 20 miles away. There was no swimming pool close, and if you went to the pool you had to have money to go in. So that was knocked on the head.

Hilary's mother restricted her movements, not allowing her to wander around the neighbourhood. Unlike in the old days when they could 'take off to the bush' in Mt Druitt they were not allowed to stray beyond the end of the street. The area lacked amenities; no local shops or community centres. Hilary felt marooned on the bare sunbaked acres of the outer west, deprived of the freedoms that she had grown used to:

> It was all clay. There was no grass put down. So you had the hose running just to make a mud pie. And plus the transport was pretty well lax, because the nearest town was St. Marys itself ... A fair way to walk. And if you haven't got your own car, you had to rely on public transport. And the nearest bus stop was about a kilometre away.

Her father was employed in 'different odd jobs' in the Penrith area and he had to rise very early to get to work. Her mother, with responsibility for several young children, was largely restricted to the home. She had to travel by taxi to and from St Marys to shop.

Like Millicent, Hilary recalls that Aboriginal families were dispersed across the large expanses of Mt Druitt. Her family had only non-Indigenous neighbours and she felt resentful that they had been drawn into a situation where they felt pressure to match the living standards of their neighbours:

> And then all of a sudden going to this new place, and this new house, and even though we had the running water and the electricity, and the lovely home. In the early days I hated living there, because you know

> with the new home, you have to have new carpets, new curtains, and see Mum and Dad just didn't have the money to do that. So we had sheets up at the window, and we had bare floorboards, and just none of the ... trappings of being in a new home in suburbia.

She felt the shame of poverty very keenly in these vulnerable teenage years:

> All I can remember is that all of the neighbours around us, had all the trappings. You know they all had lovely new curtains, new lino or new carpet .... I felt shamed about inviting friends back home, because we had bare floorboards, and sheets at the windows and all that type of stuff. And I gathered that their place had all the nice trimmings of a new home ... But then after a period of time, we did get all the trappings of a new home, but I don't know how long it took.

Hilary had contact with few other Aboriginal people in the area outside her own family. Eventually another large Aboriginal family moved into a house in the next street. The children were a similar age to Hilary and her siblings and they became life-long friends after that. When she reached high-school age, Hilary was forced to commute for more than an hour each morning and afternoon to Rooty Hill because there was no high school in Mt Druitt. It was at this time that Hilary first remembers confronting racism:

> These boys walked past, and they said something about me being an 'abo' or 'coon'. And I just questioned why they wanted to talk to me like that, because I didn't say anything then. They just blurted it out, and I didn't say anything to Mum or Dad.

Nevertheless, the members of her small group of school friends were all non-Indigenous. The only other Aboriginal student she recalls meeting was a girl who had been fostered by white people.

Like many Aboriginal men Hilary's father died young, in his early fifties in 1971. This event intensified the poverty that the family was already experiencing. There was a delay of about seven weeks before Hilary's mother was able to receive the widows' pension. In the meantime the family had to rely on charities to provide them with boxes of food which were delivered to their house. She remembers running down the road to meet the delivery truck, excited by the prospect of having her hunger alleviated.

They fell behind in rent and electricity payments. Hilary has strong memories of the Housing Commission officers – known to her as 'long socks' because they wore shorts with long 'walk' socks – coming to their door to collect rent on Saturday mornings, clipboards in hand:

> You would see the Housing Commission car pull up at the top of the street. If you didn't have the rent to pay, you would all take off. Or make out that you weren't home, but not only us, but everyone knew how to play that game. So in those days you never went to the office and paid rent. The Housing Officer used to come to you, he would have a set number of streets every Saturday, and just walk around and collect the rent of people, and issue receipts.

When her father died Hilary was 16 and in Year 10, about to commence her junior high school examinations. Her mother asked her to leave school immediately on economic and family support grounds:

> This happens a lot in Koori families. If you're the eldest at home or you're going to school, you're expected to stay home and help out with the younger ones, and that's what happened with me.

By this stage all Hilary's older siblings had left home. She helped her mother out during the day and worked as a babysitter for local families virtually every night. She would always hand over the five dollars nightly babysitting earnings to her mother. Hilary had very little money to spend on herself. As with most young women the fantasy images held up in popular culture served as a galling counterpoint to her own material situation:

> We used to get bags of clothes dropped off too. That's what I hated too, the fact that we had to pick our clothes out from all these second-hand stuff. I used to drool over all those magazines, that had flash clothes in it, and

knowing that I could never ever buy them. I think that affected my self-esteem too. Because I had friends around with all the latest gear ...

Hilary recalls feeling ashamed when the vehicle emblazoned with the Smith Family charity name pulled up in front of her house. Like her family, a few non-Indigenous families in her area were extremely poor – they would help each other out with food when money was short – but the majority appeared to Hilary to enjoy better circumstances than those of her own.

In 1972 at her mother's prompting Hilary enrolled in a secretarial course. There followed a public-service job which required Hilary to commute the considerable distance into the centre of Sydney. She found the travel taxing on her health and when a workmate told her that she had a vacant room in her flat, she decided to move out. She recalls being very apprehensive about this development in her life. She had never been away from home and had always lived amidst the noise and chaos of her family. In the flat she had a room of her own for the first time and was disconcerted by the quiet and solitude.

Later Hilary undertook tertiary study and worked as a university administrator and then a lecturer in an Aboriginal education centre. She married, had one child, a son, and like several of her siblings, obtained a Commission dwelling. She lives in the same house in Green Valley near Liverpool that she moved into in 1981. Hilary's mother is still alive as are all but one of her siblings.

Keith

Keith, born in Griffith of Wiradjuri parents in 1950, moved to Sydney when he was young at the point where his mother Tilda separated from his father. He spoke to me broadly about his life but it is his reflections on the life of his mother Tilda, and the decisions she made to distance herself and her children from their extended family, that is of most significance. Tilda, like Hilary's mother, had front-line experience of urban assimilationist pressures. She dealt with those pressures, however, in a very different way.

Keith has very hazy memories of his early childhood that was spent in and around Cowra. Throughout our conversation he struggled to order the narrative of his life chronologically interestingly reflecting traditional

Aboriginal narrative forms in which spatial/geographical referents are more important that temporal ones. He contrasted himself with his non-Aboriginal wife:

> My memory isn't related to events. It's not a chronological memory, in terms of dates. I can remember events. I can remember places ... My wife is non-Aboriginal. She can say yes that was where the children had their first teeth. I don't relate to things like that. I can remember them having their first teeth but I can't remember chronologically.

He believes that he spent a little time living on a reserve ('Either Cowra or Allambie. Or down around Wagga, somewhere like that') but Tilda strenuously resisted settling there on a long-term basis. She yearned for social improvement and while her husband wanted to maintain closer contacts with relatives, including those on the reserve, she resisted mixing with the people who lived there because she felt they would 'get caught up with the wrong crowd':

> Mum tells a classic story ... about how they had a place with hessian walls and dirt floors. He [Dad] said 'You've got a house what more do you want?' And she wants something with floorboards, she wanted something with a roof. Like she could stay in with her kids ... The other big thing with her has been all through our lives is education ... they are the two things which have driven Mum.

They moved away from Cowra in the late 1950s to Katoomba in the Blue Mountains, west of Sydney. At this point Keith's parents were separated. His father worked as a fruit picker (in Young harvesting cherries and in the Riverina, grapes), and did basic labouring work where he could get it. He was away for extended periods like many Aboriginal men who worked as itinerate agricultural workers or on the railways. Tilda had told her husband that she was taking the children to live in Katoomba in order to 'set up a life properly'. She gave him the option of going with them but said that if he chose not to he would not be welcome to do so later on. Keith recalls returning from Katoomba to live briefly back in Cowra around 1960. In 1961, however, Tilda went to the city for a throat operation, and she, Keith, his two younger brothers and a sister remained in the Sydney region for the rest of his childhood.

Tilda burned her bridges. She had absorbed the assimilationist notion that Aboriginal culture and community was incompatible with a comfortable modern urban lifestyle and wanted no aspect of her old way of life to intrude upon the future. Keith's father eventually moved to Sydney to work for a printing company in the mid 1970s, when the downturn in the rural economy reduced the demand for agricultural labour. However, he was never reunited with Tilda and died in 1990.

They had no relatives in Sydney at the time of their arrival. Tilda placed Keith's two younger brothers in an orphanage boys' home at Kincumber near Gosford (a place with 'not a very good reputation ... with Aboriginal children'), probably in response to the social and economic difficulties associated with relocating. At first Keith stayed with his mother during 1961, briefly attending Parramatta Public School, but then was placed at Boystown, in Engadine, in Sydney's far southern suburbs. His sister had been at Kelso near Bathurst but moved to be with their mother from 1962. He cannot remember why he was not at first located in the same orphanage as his brothers but they were eventually moved to Boystown. He recalls the years there with no great fondness but neither were they particularly miserable times. He gained a lot of self-esteem as a result of his prowess in sport. The children would sometimes see their mother during holidays. She lived in private rental accommodation in Wentworthville in the western suburbs. Keith saw his father only very occasionally at this time.

Eventually Tilda rented a house at Dee Why on Sydney's northern beaches. She brought her three sons to stay with her during the September school holidays in 1965. The boys were enjoying their break immensely. When Tilda contacted Boystown to tell them the children would be staying longer than she had at first told them, she was officiously informed that she was obliged to return them. Tilda reacted angrily to this direction and spontaneously put it to the children that they remain living with her. Keith and his siblings received this suggestion enthusiastically and so the family was reunited.

In November 1965 the family were offered a three-bedroom bungalow in Green Valley. Keith described Green Valley in terms similar to those used by Hilary and Millicent in their recollections of Mt Druitt. The area lacked community facilities. It was a landscape of 'baking hard claypan soil ... not as bushed up as it is now' and completely devoid of the services and facilities that serve as the mortar of community. Nevertheless this was the realisation of a dream for Tilda:

> To Mum at this stage it was the culmination of everything we wanted ... It must have been difficult for Mum ... There has been a very conscious decision by her to walk away from some aspect of her cultural background, and that is to see the mission as dirty and untidy. It may have had aspect of behaviour there with my father, and what was going on and drinking and that kind of thing. It may have affected her life and his. I don't know enough about it. But I do know that she had a very strong cultural severance at that time.

Unlike Hilary and Millicent, Keith had little experience of extended family coming to stay in his mother's house. His mother made it quite clear that she did not 'want particular kinds of people around'. Much later Tilda's sisters came to live in Sydney, but they were less close than is common in Aboriginal families.

Keith was keenly aware that his mother was (and still is) insecure about her Aboriginality. She has apparently internalised the negative evaluations of the era:

> You know where you go out and you don't go down the street untidy because we are not going to be seen with those kind of black people who just go down the streets of Redfern.

Many Indigenous women of Tilda's generation were haunted by these spectres, desperate to be seen as respectable and worthy. Keith suggested obliquely that she was unable to speak publicly as an Aboriginal person:

> ... it's only been the last couple of years that she can stand up, and even then still finds it difficult ... People of that generation still find it difficult to stand up and make statements.

He describes her as houseproud but he considered this to be 'negative' because he saw her as doing this in order to meet the expectations of others rather than for the intrinsic satisfaction of creating a clean and ordered home.

Keith recalls Green Valley at this time as being a place of poverty and struggle where most of the non-Indigenous working-class families were in the same situation as his own. He went to Ashcroft High School and apart from hearing occasional racist gibes from passing school children ('blackfella, that sort of thing') had very little sense of being different from the majority. Keith excelled in sport and was generally popular amongst his peers. He completed the Higher School Certificate (HSC) in 1969 and achieved a moderate pass but did not meet the standard required for university entry. His attendance patterns had been particularly poor leading up to the examinations and he now thinks that he did not really understand why he was doing them ('I didn't know what happened beyond the HSC'). By this time his sister had left home and he was probably called up to assist his mother on many occasions.

At this point he was taken under the wing of the Aboriginal Education Council, a body that supported Indigenous students. Keith was persuaded to do the HSC again with the offer of a scholarship sponsored by the Waterside Workers Federation, a radical union. Similar assistance was also offered to his two brothers. Tilda had severe misgivings about her sons receiving this assistance, believing that they would incur obligations to a communist organisation later on. More disturbing for her, however, was that Keith was encouraged to move to a new school, one where his prospects would be likely to improve. He attended Marsden High School during 1970 and was taken away to board with a white family which his benefactors believed would provide him with a better environment for study. In the days before Aboriginal politics was guided by the ethic of self-determination there were many such philanthropically inclined people who sought to assist Indigenous children. Charity, however, can often leave scars and even though Keith matriculated and was offered a place in Engineering at Sydney University, his mother was deeply disturbed by the process. She had struggled for social mobility, willingly sacrificed her ties to community and, in spite of all of this, she was deemed to be unable to provide a home environment conducive to her children achieving their potential:

> Mum carries some pretty emotional scars over that time ... The actual process of going to another school and doing well was not the problem. It was that the home environment was perceived to be the problem.

Keith began his university course in 1971 but struggled from the outset. In those days there were very few support structures for Aboriginal students and again he had very little idea of the purpose of his course. He left the next year. In 1974 he got married to a non-Indigenous woman whom he had started going out with while at Marsden High. He was employed in a department store and they rented a flat for three years before buying another at Granville. At the time he had 'no concept' of home ownership but was persuaded into it by his wife. When they were able to sell the property three years later for twice the price Keith was surprised and intrigued that this process could happen. This was indicative of his own social mobility. Unlike most Aboriginal people at this time Keith bought property early in his adult life. Perhaps if he had not taken the path mapped out for him by the Aboriginal Education Council, from Green Valley to the North Shore to university, his life would have taken a very different course. After selling their flat Keith and his wife decided to move away from Sydney. They both craved rural life and purchased 100 acres near Lithgow to the west of the city.

Like his mother Keith has never been strongly connected to his Aboriginal community of origin. At one stage he was teaching in the jail system and there he came across several relatives, cousins who were serving terms of imprisonment, and who had the kind of extensive genealogical knowledge which is typical of many Indigenous people. In the 1980s Keith became involved with a Lands Council and was elected an office bearer. He later studied law.

Joyce

Joyce was born in 1947. She had an Aboriginal father and a mother, born in Australia, of Anglo background. Her father was from Bourke and had moved to the Sydney area in the late 1930s, before the main wave of Aboriginal migration. He came in search of work and also to escape the poverty that blighted his home community. She remembers being told by her father that Bourke was a place of chronic alcoholism 'where everyone dealt with their problems by drinking'.

Joyce's first home was Merrylands that today forms part of Sydney's western suburbs but which at the time was largely rural. It was a place of desolation and isolation with 'no sewerage, no public transport, no nothing'. Her father worked in a battery factory during World War Two and, because this was an essential industry, he could not be called up for active service. He was very successful in his work, was well regarded by his employers and eventually became a foreman. Joyce recalls her mother telling her that the family had the opportunity to purchase the house they lived in at Merrylands but that because of her father's reluctance to settle in the one spot, they declined to do so. He eventually lost his job in the factory 'because of the alcohol'.

From this point Joyce's life became peripatetic. Her parents took Joyce and her two older brothers, one of whom was intellectually disabled, to live in rental accommodation in various locations in and around Sydney. From Merrylands they moved to the western suburbs of Drummoyne, then to Rosehill, and then to the Blue Mountains to the west of Sydney where they lived in several locations. This constant movement was largely the result of Joyce's father's drinking and his failure to hold down a job. He also had 'the whole domestic violence situation, the whole gamut that goes with people with alcoholic problems'.

She remembers that her parents told her to conceal her Aboriginality where possible in order to improve her life chances. She was to some extent able to do this because of her fair skin. Her eldest (intellectually disabled) brother was also fair skinned but her middle brother and her father were dark skinned:

> We would be asked were we Italian because, you know, the darkness. So you would get away better by saying yes you had Italian descent, than Aboriginal.

Like many who endeavoured to pass, Joyce never brought friends home from school. Nor did her middle brother who was unable to hide his Aboriginality and suffered racist persecution. As a consequence he rebelled:

> He was more discriminated against, all the way through at school, teachers, shopkeepers ... and ended up in jail. Horrific. But he sort of wore it all.

At the time when her parents married there were powerful social taboos against such mixed unions. Joyce recalls her mother telling her that she felt that their love would help them overcome the social barriers and prejudice. There was, however, enormous pressure from members of her mother's family who had opposed the marriage:

> I can remember relatives in the home, and because Dad did have a drinking problem. I can remember all the relatives saying to my mother 'we told you from the beginning not to marry him. We told you that it wouldn't work, it is your own fault that you are living the life that you are. You should never have married him, he's black, they can't change' ... They all tried their best for her to leave him. They resented every child she ever had.

Nevertheless Joyce recalls that her aunts and grandmother were prepared to take her out shopping with them because she was fair. They refused, however, to take her dark-skinned brother because 'they didn't want people to look at him'.

Joyce's father told her that his family also would also not have approved of the union. He refused to return to Bourke with his wife because he felt that his relatives would not accept her because she was white, 'so they were caught in the middle of two cultures'. Nevertheless the respective families occasionally visited them when they lived in the Blue Mountains, but never together. ('You would always had to have a visit with the white family, and then you had a visit with the black family. There was no middle ground'.)

Joyce's mother was a fastidious housekeeper and never allowed her children to go out unless they were 'spotless'. She kept up appearances even when the family was living in sub-standard housing:

> When we lived in the mountains, we lived in a shack, it was three rooms, no running water, you went out to the front tap for water. No lights, no bath ... She made curtains for it. I can remember we didn't

have any paint, and we didn't have any money for paint. So she got whitewash, and put the blue dye that you put in the sheets to make the sheets white, she dyed the whitewash blue, and we painted all the outside of this shack blue. And it looked beautiful. She would adapt to make do.

It was common for working-class women to strive to present a respectable face to the world. Because Joyce's mother was married to an Aboriginal man she worked even harder to convey an image of moral and domestic rectitude.

There was also, however, a darker fear that her parents held during the 1950s when Joyce was growing up:

> Well my mum said, and my dad said too, 'that if we [don't put on our best appearance], they would come and take the children away'. He said 'everything has got to be just right, because if one person in the street says anything, because I am black, they will come and take the children away, and say we are not looking after them properly'.

Joyce believes that her father's reluctance to settle in one place was in part a consequence of his efforts to evade the surveillance of the state. He was convinced, with good reason, that official scrutiny of the domestic life of his family would lead to his children being removed. He moved to Sydney and when his children were born, he vowed he would never return to Bourke. Joyce remembers him saying that he could get lost in the city and escape the regulation of the state and minimise the possibility of having his children removed. He lived like a fugitive:

> In a sense he was in jail, because he was Aboriginal, and if he dared have children ... if he slipped up they could come and take those kids away from him. And even when two of the children came out white, he said, I can remember Dad, and he had a few drinks and he would say 'they will take you, you know, they will get you. Because you could be adopted out, and you could live with a white family, and no one would know. So they would take you, before they take [my dark-skinned brother].

After 25 years of marriage, Joyce's mother decided she could not endure the family situation any more. They had severe financial problems largely as a result of her husband's drinking. While living in the mountains she had established a small business slaughtering and dressing chickens and making brawn for sale to butchers. She also grew and sold fruit and vegetables. This enabled her to save enough to give her a degree of financial independence. Then, in spite of her love for her husband, she left him and took the children from the Blue Mountains to live back in Drummoyne with Joyce's grandmother. Joyce was 12 at this time. She last saw her father when she was 15.

At first after moving to Drummoyne Joyce's mother could not find a job. She eventually found work as a cleaner and later as a shop assistant, struggling for every penny to enable her to support the three children. These were years of severe poverty. Joyce was obliged to leave school at 15 to earn a living.

At around about this time they applied for Housing Commission accommodation. At first they were rejected on the grounds that they were adequately housed in the grandmother's three-bedroom house. They protested stating that Joyce's disabled brother needed a bedroom for himself and did not have one in Drummoyne. The Commission relented and granted them housing. At no stage did Joyce's mother identify herself as Aboriginal in order to try to obtain priority because she felt that after she left her husband 'she wasn't entitled to any help at all'. This was before the introduction of the HFA scheme but at the point where the Housing Commission was settling some 'model' Aboriginal families in Housing Commission estates.

They moved into a two-bedroom house in Green Valley when Joyce was 17:

> I can remember when the Department of Housing rung and told us we had the house. And [my mother] said 'everyone is telling me that I should go and look at it, but I'm not going to look at it. I don't care what it's like, it's a home and I want a home for my children, and home is where the heart is'. So she took it, sight unseen. She said 'I'm not knocking anything back'. She said 'I'm lucky to get it and I'll have it'. So we came up and moved in the day we saw it.

Joyce felt euphoric at moving into the house even though the living conditions were cramped. Joyce's eldest brother required a room of his own because of his disability (the middle brother had left home at this point) and at first Joyce was forced to share a bedroom with her mother. She married at 19 but continued to live with her mother.

Green Valley was bare and lacking resources: few buses and shops, no trees. Like the other interviewees Joyce recalls the baking clay and the treeless expanses of the suburbs. Her mother, however, saw the bright side of things:

> It was sewered and guttered. And Mum said that we were well off, because we had gutters ... everywhere we lived except for Drummoyne. I mean Merrylands was no sewer. The mountains ... [had] no sewer. So Mum thought that we were very well off to have sewer. We had luxury.

Most of those who moved to the area in the 1960s were thrilled to be given a house and garden at a time when there was an enormous shortage of housing. Many young families had been lodging with relatives in cramped quarters in the inner city. Public housing was their salvation.

Today Joyce identifies as Aboriginal. She no longer experiences that sense of shame that she felt earlier. She is active in Aboriginal organisations and works in community welfare where she deals with many Aboriginal clients. She is also active in local government. She regrets that her mother, who died of cancer aged 56, just before the birth of Joyce's second child, did not live long enough to share the easier and more financially secure life which Joyce has enjoyed in recent times.

Common Threads – Comparing the Narratives

The life patterns of the four interviewees are typical of Indigenous Australians in the post-war period. They were pushed from the bush by poverty, lack of work, racism, and drawn to the city by the prospect of better jobs and services. The routes were diverse. Keith's mother and Joyce's father burned bridges or at least put physical and cultural distance between themselves and their families. Hilary's family left their home town when the work for her father dried up, Millicent's family travelled to Sydney in search of a better life – education, housing and so on. Also, like many of her people, Millicent commuted frequently between country and city, both as a child and adult.

These are narratives of migration. Many of those who came to Australia as migrants or refugees from overseas in the fifties and sixties were accommodated in hostels and received forms of state assistance to help them in their process of cultural adjustment. No significant public support was available to Aboriginal people even though they too experienced displacement, upheaval and a process of cultural disorientation. Although they did not cross national borders, Indigenous people traversed other symbolic lines.

Many of the habits of life characteristic of suburban areas were unfamiliar. The interviewees described problems of cultural translation. How would you translate your experiences on a reserve, or living in a makeshift dwelling on a farm or a riverbank camp, to develop a sense of what was required of you on a Housing Commission estate? Millicent recalled her failure to recognise the importance of maintaining the outward appearance of her home. Keith spoke of his inability to grasp the purpose and value of achieving good results in school. Hilary remembered being puzzled and resentful because her neighbours fenced off their land and she was confined to her family's quarter-acre block. These examples indicate the conflict and dissonance between Aboriginal ways and those of the social mainstream. A former reserve dweller could see little point in spending hours cultivating and tending to a front garden. Someone who knew nothing of universities or academic credentialing processes could see little point in competing with other students for high marks – competitive individualism is not a natural condition of all human society but an ideological construction of our own.

After generations of being told that their culture and ways of life were worthless and primitive, and that they should aspire to live like white people in cities and towns, most Aboriginal people naturally felt exposed and inadequate when they moved into suburban housing. The great majority sensed that they were being judged by neighbours and Commission officers on the basis of their Aboriginality; that they were expected to trip up, to relapse into the wayward habits of the 'fringe dweller'. Women, as those held most directly accountable for standards of family respectability, were constantly working against this stereotype, as the testimony of all four interviewees demonstrates. They struggled assiduously to keep their houses cleaner than those around them. They dressed their children neatly and respectably. They were strong and held families together, often in situations where their husbands were alcoholics.

The environment of the Housing Commission estate heightened this sense of inadequacy. The older spatial solidarities of the reserve and the inner city were broken down. If proximity to relatives bred solidarity it also bred poverty. To the Aboriginal arrivals, the new estates did not appear to be communities of poverty in the same way as their older residential settings. Deprivation was better concealed. The emphasis was on cultivating an appearance of middle classness based on the nuclear family. The insecurities of Aboriginal tenants resulted from the pressures they experienced that were based on class and gender as well as race. As new tenants they were inserted into an environment designed to eradicate certain forms of class behaviour. They were expected to refrain from hosting loud parties that were disruptive of neighbourhood peace and order, to prevent their front gardens from becoming overgrown and thereby destroying the order and regularity of the suburb streetscape. They were expected to respect the sanctity of neighbours' homes by preventing their children from rampaging through adjacent gardens. However, the general racist inference which informed the practice of the Housing Commission and, doubtless, the attitude of many fellow tenants was that Aboriginal people would be unable to progress beyond the standards of the undeserving poor–that they were constitutionally unable to demonstrate the requisite respectability, conformity and restraint.

The narratives demonstrate that there were degrees of identification or concealment of Aboriginality amongst those who lived on suburban estates. Joyce's family were certainly keen to conceal the Indigenous background of her father. Hilary's family did not seek to pass. Millicent did not wish to distance herself from relatives but found it hard to maintain the contact without making the effort to return to her old haunts. She may well have been viewed, like many of those who moved into suburban housing, as an 'uptown black' (pejorative term used against Aboriginal people deemed socially mobile and aloof) by her people in the inner city and become slightly alienated from them as a result. Tilda clearly experienced great ambivalence about Aboriginality. While not denying it completely, she apparently bought into an ideology of individualism, following the pattern of those who endeavour to 'pull themselves up by their bootstraps' and renounce those whom they have left behind. Those who make such a choice effectively deny themselves the opportunity of interpreting any misfortune they suffer themselves as being the result of discrimination or disempowerment. Hence she was bewildered at being seen as unable to provide a home suitable for cultivating Keith's intellectual gifts. We might understand, but not necessarily sympathise with, her frustration at not being accepted as worthy, despite her efforts to claw her way out of poverty. Tilda was caught in the cleft stick that catches so many of those who pursue social mobility.

Each of the four narratives outlined above contains a description of relationship breakdown or bereavement. Hilary's father died young, Joyce's and Keith's mothers left their husbands, Millicent separated from the father of her children. Such events are the norm rather than the exception in Aboriginal families. The pattern of early death, particularly amongst Indigenous men, and the tendency for men to desert their partners, meant that many children had very little time to get to know their fathers before they disappeared from their lives.

The Housing Commission tenancy system provided a safety net. The cataclysmic effect of bereavement or separation was mitigated because it was possible for tenancies to be continued and for rent – calculated as a percentage of income – to be reduced. There were numerous examples contained in the Housing Commission files of tenancies being transferred to be in the sole name of the custodial parent upon death or separation. For all of those interviewed, with the exception of Millicent who moved into private ownership, the Housing Commission family home, whether theirs or their parents', was a point of anchorage and stability. Hilary, Joyce and Keith each described disrupted periods in their lives being brought to an end when their parents successfully obtained Commission housing. For all of its problems then, the tenancy system provided a bulwark against misfortune.

Many Aboriginal suburban dwellers strove to keep their identity and culture alive in the crucible of suburban moral respectability. But it is important to see the public and political dimensions of this struggle. In the next chapter I will argue that Aboriginality is not something that is singular, fixed and constant but is constructed and reconstructed in the shifting social and political conditions of post-war Australia. We can see evidence of this transition in the oral testimony of Hilary, Millicent, Joyce and Keith. They spoke to me at a point in history where public regard for Aboriginal culture and recognition of the hardships they have suffered, were higher than in the past. The contemporary emergence of the politics of pan-Aboriginality has provided those living in the city with unifying symbols. This politics has also furnished a collective basis for their claims to Indigenous identity and provided at least some public acknowledgment of the sorts of life experiences they have had. Although, as we shall see in the next chapter, the dominant public depictions of Aboriginal traditionalism are still a very limiting force, it is not only those living in remote settings who can confidently claim Indigenous credentials. In recalling situations where they felt out of place or were unable to meet social expectations, the interviewees have developed the resources to understand this awkwardness. Such reflections can generate feelings ranging from wry amusement to intense anger. Whatever emotions are generated, it is clear only when the life circumstances being described have been transcended that those who experienced them can obtain a critical distance. The distance which my interviewees (particularly Hilary and Millicent) have been able to obtain is produced from their current greater sense of ease and confidence about cultural difference.

Conclusion

The material explored in this chapter indicates that Aboriginality is not simply a shared history and a cultural inheritance. It is a contemporary identity position that provides a means for ordering and interpreting life courses, for structuring and encoding biographical narratives. The dominant public narratives of post-war Australia stressed individual achievement, consumption and family values. These were framed around the idea of the liberal subject striving for social advancement and prosperity in a society where people were told that opportunities were available to those with talents. We can see how structured circumstances affected the lives of the people discussed in this chapter so as to cleave personal from public narratives.

Where collective responsibilities, the racist practice of public officials or ideological marginalisation intruded on the lives of Indigenous people they were unable to meet bourgeois-individual expectations. Contemporary pan-Aboriginality has endowed Aboriginal people, particularly those in cities, with a critical and political hindsight, albeit one that is often reductive in foregrounding colonial relations at the expense of those of class and gender. Hilary was frustrated that the glamour she saw in magazines was always out of reach for a girl in a large Koori family where there was never enough to go around. Millicent strove to find some representation of herself and her people in the school curriculum but found instead that Aboriginality was expressed only in images of noble savagery. Keith was perplexed that teachers and mentors were pushing him to compete against other children in school assessment and could see no tangible benefit from doing so.

We have seen here that the narratives of modernism were inflexible and the instruments of assimilation were blunt. In the era in which my interviewees grew up there was very little space for those from minority backgrounds to negotiate the meritocratic narratives that were unrolled before them. There was no room for counter narratives in which collective responsibilities might cut across the performance of conventional suburban lifestyles. Through its petty officials the modernist state preached at, hectored and shamed those subjects who diverged from social norms. But the force of public example was not sufficiently strong to secure social conformity. The vernacular and collective cultural forms endured in places where they were least expected to do so. In the next chapter I will consider the nature of Aboriginal identity in the light of the experience of urbanisation.

Chapter 6

Contemporary Aboriginalities

The Indigenous social order in Australia has withstood the process of urbanisation despite the blowtorch colonial authorities applied to Aboriginal culture.[1] This chapter will consider contemporary Indigenous urban identity. In the first chapter I argued that cultures are never completely discrete (Bakhtin 1994) and that no culture survives in a state of petrified tradition, notwithstanding the reverence that may exist for that tradition. In the words of Marcia Langton Aboriginality 'is remade over and over again in a process of dialogue, of imagination, of representation and interpretation. Both Aboriginal and non-Aboriginal people create "Aboriginalities" ... in the infinite array of intercultural experiences' (Langton 1993, p. 34). At various times and places colonial/settler ideology in Australia has cast Indigenous people in a range of roles – the noble savage, the vicious and demoralised fringe dweller, the child-like subject of state and missionary paternalism. Although Aboriginal people have resisted these representations they endure even where the social conditions on which they were founded have dissolved. Echoes can be found today in official discourse and the media (Langton 1993). While images of Indigenous tradition have a central place in the ideas of nationhood, contemporary Aboriginalities remain much more marginal. In their engagement with broader society, in a public sense, many Aboriginal urban dwellers embrace primordial symbols of their collective selves. In this chapter I will consider why this is so and whether, as Povinelli suggested in a recent book, 'hegemonic domination ... works primarily by inspiring in the Indigenous subject a desire to identify with a lost indeterminate object – indeed to be the melancholic subject of traditions' (Povinelli 2002, p. 39).

Classifying Aboriginality

What are the foundations of contemporary urban Aboriginal identity claims? The definition, classification and management of Aboriginality were central to the administration of Aboriginal affairs in the period when authorities believed they were overseeing the demise of Aboriginality (McGregor 1997). In the early twentieth century Aboriginality was calculated by measure of blood. Those deemed 'part-Aboriginal' were separated from their full-blood kin on the assumption that they were more able to be assimilated. Fair-skinned children were deemed to be of lesser Aboriginal blood (this was usually an arbitrary process of classification not based on genealogical investigation) and were more vulnerable to being taken away from their parents. In Australia today there is no requirement for claimants to establish that a particular proportion of their forebears were Indigenous in order to gain official recognition. There is general acceptance amongst Aboriginal people today that Aboriginality is indivisible and there is great hostility to the idea of creating hierarchies according to measure of blood. This vast majority of those identifying as Indigenous have some non-Indigenous forebears, particularly amongst the highly urbanised communities of the more densely populated south east. In the past, those who were the product of mixed unions – more often European fathers and Aboriginal mothers than vice versa – were much more likely to be embraced by, and therefore to identify with, their Indigenous rather than their European extended families. So 'blood' had very little to do with how much someone identified with, and was accepted by, a particular Indigenous community and experienced the associated oppression.

From the mid-twentieth century authorities switched from biological to cultural yardsticks for measuring Aboriginality. Authenticity was based on familiarity with traditions – language, law, lore, ritual. This excluded those who wished to identify but who through the operation of colonialism had been denied their communal heritage because:

a) in the face of cultural shaming elders were often reluctant to share traditional knowledge with young people
b) children were removed from their parents and deprived of the chance of cultural initiation
c) many Aboriginal people were removed from their land and lost the spiritual bearings that it provided to them.

This cultural persistence approach defined Aboriginal culture as a vestige and implied a zero sum relationship with 'mainstream' culture – that those who are drawn into that mainstream necessarily underwent a depletion of their Indigenous identity (Chase 1981).

A much more inclusive approach to Aboriginality incorporates the possibility of cultural change as well as continuity, accepting the role of contemporary process in the formation of identity (Hollinsworth 1996). Aboriginality is not simply a vestige of something that has survived from the past. Like all cultures it is formed in a process of dialogue, engagement and resistance and involves the incorporation of elements of the cultures of the colonisers. Aboriginal culture, from this point of view, has prospective as well as retrospective elements. This approach avoids fixed classifications of identity. It allows for an understanding of, and validates the development of, a pan-Aboriginality instead of leading towards a fragmented localised communal politics, such as is implied by definitions based on traditional cultural identity. It also permits non-Indigenous people more scope for participation in anti-colonial movements by avoiding defining racial politics around fixed, segregated and incommensurable communities.

This open-ended approach to Aboriginality is similar to ideas about black identity that have been developed in cultural theory in Britain and the US (Hall 1992). It provides a place for those who are not steeped in traditions and confronts what Paul Gilroy calls 'cultural insiderism', whereby those with greater knowledge of traditions can claim a higher place in the communal pecking order (Gilroy 1987 as cited in Hollinsworth 1996). Indigenous pluralism means that cultural initiation and tutelage from elders is not essential to authenticating the identity claims of urban Aboriginal people. As Hall points out, transcultural movement and mixing 'has made ethnic absolutism an increasingly untenable cultural strategy' (Hall 1996, p. 250).

The debates around contemporary Indigenous identity and culture parallel those that refer to the experiences of people from colonised nations of the Third World who have migrated to the cities of the West. Much of this debate has taken place around the concept of post-colonialism, originally a term used by Marxist writers to describe the political, economic and historical dimensions of decolonisation, but in recent times referring to cultural processes (Ahmad 1995). Rattansi (1997) defines post-colonial studies as:

> the investigation of the mutually constitutive role played by coloniser and colonised, centre and periphery, the metropolitan and the 'native', in forming, in part, the identities of both the dominant power and the subalterns involved in the imperial and colonial projects of the West.

Colonial and Indigenous cultures intertwine and colonised people absorb some of the language, practices and symbolic structures of the dominant culture (Thomas 1991). Conversely, as Bhabha argues, the presence of native people simultaneously undermines colonialism, holding up the mirror to the coloniser, shattering the comfortable illusions of tradition, the pretensions of cultural superiority and drawing attention to the fractured underside of colonial life (Bhabha 1985). For post-colonialists there is no cultural or physical boundary between the Indigenous and the colonial, no interior and exterior.

Other commentators have questioned the assumption that colonised peoples willingly embrace the possibilities offered by global and metropolitan culture. Friedman, for example, has criticised the tendency for middle-class intellectuals from colonised countries to assume that their celebration of complex, hybrid cultural identities is necessarily shared by poor migrants (Friedman 1994). He claims that the great majority of those who live on the social margins have neither the possibility nor the desire to be culturally eclectic, to engage in a playful and self-reflexive process of identity formation. They are much more inclined to hold onto tradition than the post-colonialists would suppose. Brennan supports this observation:

> Lost in much of the writing on colonialism and post colonialism is the mood of languorous attachment to native cultures ... If hybridity can be said to characterise them, then it is a hybridity reclaimed and reinvented as Indigenous, defiantly posed against an increasingly insistent metropolitan norm (Brennan 1997).

Although Brennan was writing about immigrants in the United States, his observations could apply equally to most Aboriginal people living in

Australia's towns and cities. Educated, prosperous, middle-class members of ethnic minorities may feel free to explore cultural possibilities, to articulate innovative versions of their collective identities based on combining contemporary and traditional forms. But for the most part urban Aboriginal people are not in such a situation. They are generally poor and socially marginal and like most people in such situations they embrace traditional symbols of their collective selves.

This presents something of a paradox because Aboriginal people in cities appear to have much to lose by flying the flag of Indigenous tradition. They are engaged in what Spivak calls strategic essentialism, a pragmatic politics employed by cultural minorities in opposition to a disorganising colonialism (Spivak 1988). This means that expressions of Aboriginality in everyday life are replete with references to ancient arrangements. For example those who live in Redfern refer to community leaders (many of whom are recognised as such even though they hold no elected office) as elders, even though their roles are very different from those of tribal elders. Many Aboriginals who have lived in cities for most or all of their lives make sense of their existence through reference to traditional social arrangements and to the nurturing and guiding properties of traditional lands and kinship links (e.g. a teenage boy who is nowhere to be found may be referred to as having 'gone walkabout'). Aboriginal writers have defended this strategy of cultural essentialism (Nyoongah 1992; Anderson 1995). Dodson argued that it was the prerogative of Aboriginal people to move between different expressions of their own identities – 'at times ancient, at times subversive, at times oppositional, at times secret, at times essentialist, at times shifting' (Dodson 1994).

Culture, Identity and Pan-Aboriginality

So what leads Aboriginal people to express their collective identities in neo-traditional terms? We saw in Chapter 3 how Indigenous migration to cities laid the foundation for new forms of Aboriginality. Jones and Hill-Burnett define this as a moment of *ethnogenesis* where pan-Aboriginal politics and culture has begun to unite the many hundreds of Aboriginal nations that pre-dated colonisation (Jones and Hill-Burnett 1992). The leaders of this movement were not simply expressing longstanding communal culture in contemporary political terms. They were engaged in a process of symbolic reconstruction and re-invention. This involved both recruiting specific localised/regional traditional culture (like dot painting, peculiar to the people of Central Australia), holding it up as being emblematic of Aboriginal people as a whole, and developing a radical politics on behalf of all Indigenous people. Those, like Millicent, Hilary, Joyce and Keith, who grew to adulthood in this era, could thereby break the ideological shackles that had been imposed on their parents' generation during the Assimilation era. The radical Indigenous movement provided them with a vantage point from which to reflect critically on their earlier life.

Those who are active in the many Aboriginal organisations that emerged in this period speak a political language that depicts Aboriginality as occupying a separate social space. They see themselves as guided by a culture and value system that is distinct from that operating in wider society ('our ways' and 'whitefella ways'). They view the process of participating in the white system as a necessary evil but as being at odds with the cooperative practices which were characteristic of traditional Indigenous social life. Traditional symbols serve to legitimate the binary divisions that are at the heart of contemporary Aboriginal community action, to overcome the threat of collapse into a homogenised and atomised politics of citizenship.

It is important to understand the subjective purchase of pan-Aboriginality for contemporary Indigenous urban dwellers. If, as Jones and Hill-Burnett argue, Aboriginal leaders were engaged in a process of defining 'a new social category' in both political and cultural terms – of inventing tradition – does this mean that contemporary Aboriginality is a mere fabrication? Dodson argues strongly against the notion of invention:

> When we talk about an Aboriginality based on the past of our peoples, we are not talking about fabricating an identity based on a past we have rediscovered or dug up ... The past cannot be limiting because we are always transforming it ... We do not need to re-find the past because our subjectivities, our being in the world are inseparable from the past. Aboriginalities of today are re-generations and transformations of the spirit of the past, not literal duplications of it (Dodson 1994, p. 10).

What is questionable in this statement is the rhetorical closure suggested by 'we'. The Australian Indigenous population is culturally complex and variegated occupying a range of life worlds from the remotest desert settlements to inner urban communities, from those conversant in traditional language and ceremony to those who lost those links generations ago. Dodson suggests that a common spirit essence overcomes this sociological diversity and unites all Indigenous peoples. As he suggests, Aboriginal lived culture involves the re-generation and transformation of inherited cultural repertoires. But when urban Indigenous people forged a sense of pan-Aboriginal identity, building a sense of being distinctive from mainstream society, they appropriated and consciously revived traditional symbols and ideas of Aboriginality that were frequently idealised and usually remote from their own life experiences.

In order to understand this process it is useful to consider Raymond Williams's ideas on cultural continuity. He suggests that social identities are shaped by the interplay of dominant, emergent and residual cultural forms. Culture, for Williams, is never static but always in the process of being made and remade. Members of marginal groups do not simply abandon their cultural inheritance when they move into new social settings. Nor do they uncritically accept dominant cultural constructions. Rather they forge their collective identities at the junction of the dominant, the residual and the emergent. Culture is a process of negotiation between the old and the new. However, Williams is keen to distinguish residual culture from the archaic:

> By residual I mean something different from the 'archaic' though in practice these are often very hard to distinguish ... I would call the 'archaic' that which is wholly recognised as an element of the past, to be observed, to be examined, or even on occasion to be consciously revived, in a deliberately specializing way. What I mean by the 'residual' is very different. The residual, by definition, has been effectively formed in the past, but is still active in the cultural process, not only and often not at all as an element of the past, but only as an effective element of the present (Williams 1977).

Jones and Hill-Burnett suggest that the process of ethnogenesis involves the revival of what are for many of those who make up the pan-Aboriginal imagined community, archaic Indigenous forms (Jones and Hill-Burnett 1992).

The important thing is that these forms do not make up the sum total of urban Indigenous cultural identity. There are indeed residual and emergent cultural forms that are authentically Indigenous even if they do not have the stamp of primordial tradition. Like the majority of global citizens, Aboriginal people produce emergent cultures from the material available through international/global culture flows. Since the 1960s, for example, young people have appropriated the symbolism of black American protest and youth cultures. Many of the land rights protestors of 30 years ago sported the Afro hairstyles, headbands and appropriated the slogans of the US Black Power movement. Today young Indigenous people embrace the styles of rap and hip-hop, and identify with the ghetto kids of New York and Los Angeles. Many young men have been inspired by the politics of Malcolm X and Louis Farrakahn. Some have converted to Islam. They are not simply cultural mimics. The motifs they adopt are given local significance. They acquire a sub-cultural meaning that is very different from that applying in the original setting.

Contemporary urban Aboriginal politics is based on the idea of a separate Indigenous community united around what are ostensibly grounding traditions. These are mainly produced though a process of contemporary re-invention to serve an existential need. For Aboriginal people living in cities and towns today ancient symbols provide a point of anchorage against the pressures to assimilate, a counterweight to bland modernity. While they practice forms of residual culture, particularly associated with familial relations, these are less visible (and less celebrated) than the unifying symbols of tradition. Fanon observed that those who live under the yoke of colonialism frequently internalise the negative evaluations which colonial ideology throws up (Fanon 1967). The stereotype of the fringe dweller, demoralised and culturally bereft, prompts Indigenous urban dwellers to seek to reconstruct aspects of the distant past rather than celebrating the residual collective forms of the present precisely because those forms do not appear sufficiently distinctive.

The Broader Context of Essentialism

In order to understand why the essential/primitive distinction dominates public understandings of Aboriginality it is necessary to look beyond the internal dynamics of Aboriginal cultural production and to grasp the general political and social processes through which this image of Aboriginality is constructed and perpetuated. Several commentators have noted that an enduring attachment to the idea of the noble savage is central to Australian national identity. Hamilton argues that Australian nationalism has long been based on a yearning for a deeper attachment to the land than non-Indigenous Australians have been able to achieve (Hamilton 1990). She claims that we have drawn on Aboriginal culture and spiritual attachment to landscape without acknowledging the debt. This has allowed us to 'claim both a mythological and spiritual continuity of identity that is otherwise lacking'.

The strategic essentialism that is often advanced by Aboriginal people is complemented (or perhaps encouraged) by a growing contemporary interest in Indigenous tradition. This is particularly characteristic of middle-class citizens of a liberal/progressive bent for whom the colonial past is a source of shame, and for those who identify with counter cultural movements. The current New Age interest in Indigenous culture is an expression of this quest for cultural purity and authenticity, for a counterweight to the shallow and ephemeral relations of modernity (for a radical critique of this see Birch 2003 and a conservative one, Sandall 2001). Indigenous tradition combines an ecological ethic with spirituality. It is untainted by modern life. This authentic culture is found in ancient places, not in cities. Tacey explores the trend to romanticise Aboriginal culture (Tacey 1995). He sees it as reflecting a popular disillusion with Western rationality and modernity and a yearning for inner spiritual fulfilment forged through a connection with nature and the land. We are, he says, engaged in a search for something that transcends the superficial and instrumental relations of our times and, as a consequence, we place Aboriginal Australia on a pedestal:

> The values of the past [have been] reversed: not we superior and they merely shadowy figures on the floor of hell, but we spiritually barren and they spiritually rich and well endowed (p. 129).

Tacey's work deals with the play of culture and ideas but not with the political dimensions of the idealisation of Aboriginality.

The concept of hegemony is useful here (Gramsci 1971). Like post-colonialism, hegemony deals with the process of cultural negotiation but it requires that culture be explored in relation to social conflict and power.

The state plays a key role as a cultural broker, in the process of defusing such conflict and in masking relations of power. Gramsci showed that the modern state struggles to win citizens over to a national-popular vision, to persuade them to identify with the 'general interest' of the nation. But in unequal societies this is difficult and involves ongoing ideological work. In the face of popular pressure the state will incorporate limited demands of disadvantaged groups into the national ideology in order to preserve the interests of powerful groups for whom it is fundamentally working. Conflict between dominant and oppressed social groups can result in pre-existing hegemonic discourse being 'abandoned as scorched earth [and] a different discourse forged in a process of disobedience and combat . . . is enunciated' (Parry 1995, p. 43). Unlike post-colonialism which encourages us to see the play of culture and power as happening without any conjunctural point of anchorage, hegemony encourages us to consider how cultural/political dynamics are institutionally marshalled.

We can see this process at work in relation to Aboriginality. In recent history the state has come to accept, and even to promote, Indigenous traditionalism largely as a hegemonic response to an Aboriginal movement that has won considerable sympathy and support for its causes within the Australian urban middle class. Two examples illustrate this shift. Firstly, there is now a considerable demand for Indigenous cultural commodities and performance such that these things are now central to the Australian tourist industry. While emergent, post-colonial, innovative cultural production is an increasingly important part of Aboriginal cultural industries, traditional (usually ersatz) representations continue to predominate, especially in catering for tourists from overseas. Povinelli states:

> As the public consumed Indigenous traditions in the form of art, music and cultural tourism, the national economy came to rely increasingly on the popularity of the simulacra of Indigenous culture to fuel the internal combustion of national private capital (Povinelli 2002, p. 50).

The Australian state, having for so long derided Aboriginal culture as primitive and worthless, now promotes airbrushed and romantic representations of that culture as central symbols of nation.

Perhaps a more important expression of hegemonic shift in relation to Aboriginality is in the field of land politics. In the Mabo and Wik decisions the Australian High Court (moved in a left-liberal direction by a series of progressive appointments in the 1980s) recognised the existence of native title and posed a challenge to mining and pastoral interests. The political and legislative response was to circumscribe those rights and to restrict the class of people who can make successful land claims. Claimants must demonstrate descent from the traditional owners of the land under claim, a continuing attachment to that land and a familiarity with traditional culture. *The Native Title Act 1993* is predicated on a notion of culture as ossified around tradition; something fixed both prior to and after colonisation (McDonald 1998). There is little scope here for those who have moved to cities and towns to argue a case for native title on the basis of residual culture in the sense that Williams uses the term. Native title law in Australia operates to exclude the great majority of those in south-eastern Australia.

Similar criteria for assessing contemporary Indigenous cultural identity applied in litigation surrounding a celebrated American native title claim that was examined by historian James Clifford (Clifford 1988). A group of people claiming to be Mashpee Indians, original owners of land that was subject to development proposals, sought legal recognition for their claims to ownership. The case hinged on whether they could establish their Indigenous bona fides: bloodlines and cultural continuity. Most of the claimants were integrated into the lives of local towns and had apparently accepted the trappings of modern life. The counsel for the developers tried to show that the claimants had lost their connection with their original culture and were simply fabricating tradition for the purpose of controlling land. The Mashpee for their part brought forward evidence of the ongoing practice of culture. Clifford accepted that some of the witnesses were involved in reinventing tradition but criticised the terms under which the case was structured. He attacked the notion that cultural authenticity is based solely on continuity and argued that culture is a living, dynamic thing rather than a vestige:

> How rooted or settled should one expect 'tribal' Native Americans to be – aboriginally in specific contact periods, and now in highly mobile twentieth-century America? Common notions of culture persistently bias the answer towards rooting rather than travel.

> Moreover the culture idea, tied as it is to assumptions about natural growth and life, does not tolerate radical breaks in historical continuity. Cultures, we often hear, 'die'. But how many cultures pronounced dead or dying by anthropologists and other authorities have, like Curtis' 'vanishing race' or Africa's diverse Christians, found new ways to be different? Metaphors of continuity and 'survival' do not account for complex historical processes of appropriation, compromise, subversion, masking, invention and revival ... The history of the Mashpee is not one of unbroken tribal institutions or cultural traditions. It is a long, relational struggle to maintain and recreate identities ... (pp. 338–339).

The claims of the Mashpee were unsuccessful. The court ruled that they had no native title rights. Clifford's observations are equally applicable to Indigenous Australians today. The production of identity is enormously complex and cannot be reduced to a notion of the endurance of the traditional into the present. It involves the articulation of archaic forms, collectively reinvented in the process of ethnogenesis, with residual forms, deeply rooted in the past but much changed from their traditional shape, and contemporary cultural materials that circulate widely in the public sphere.

The complexity of this process is lost in the mainstream idealisation of Aboriginality. For Povinelli this completely prevents positive public expressions of a contemporary Indigenous culture and identity:

> No Indigenous subject can inhabit the temporal or spatial location to which Indigenous identity refers – the geographical and social space and time of authentic Ab-originality ... Producing a present tense Indigenousness in which some failure is not a qualifying condition is discursively and materially impossible (Povinelli 2002, p. 49).

Dodson on the other hand, stresses that Aboriginal people themselves are not trapped in these public representations even if their speaking positions are circumscribed ('It's as if we've been ushered onto a stage to play in a drama where the parts have already been written'). He states that:

> we have never totally lost ourselves within the other's reality ... We have never fallen into the hypnosis of believing that those representations were our essence. Alongside the colonial discourses we have always had our own Aboriginal discourses in which we have continued to create our own representations and to recreate identities which escaped the policing of authorised versions (Dodson 1994, pp. 9–10).

This is a counterweight to Povinelli's pessimism and offers hope that the Aboriginal movement might eventually effectively marginalise the hackneyed representations of noble savagery, as many contemporary Indigenous artists and media workers are indeed seeking to do. There is clearly also scope for more ethnographic exploration of urban Aboriginality subculture: for example, its manners, ways of speaking and relating, ('yarning'), forms of gregarious enjoyment, practices of mutual support as well as the processes whereby global commodities and symbols are appropriated and given Indigenous meaning. Most Indigenous cultural production no longer takes place on traditional country but at alternative sites – at sporting carnivals, music and dance performances, on the premises of community organisations, in pubs and clubs. These are very different from the trite and romantic presentations of Aboriginality that are offered to tourists and inevitably involve ethnographers in confronting the social problems that are characteristic of contemporary Indigenous life.

Conclusion

In this chapter I have explored the way that primordial representations frame the speaking positions available to Aboriginal people themselves and the perceptions of the broader public. Traditionalism and essentialism are double-edged swords. On the one hand, they allow Indigenous city dwellers to define a distinctive space for their culture and politics to claim legitimacy based on ancient attachments. On the other hand, they have the effect of obscuring the reworked, contemporary residual forms of Indigenous culture and social life. They make urban Aboriginal people vulnerable to attacks from those who question their authenticity like Pauline Hanson and her supporters in the One Nation Party in the 1990s. They also provide a pretext for conservative politicians, like those in the Howard government, to direct Indigenous resources away from Aboriginal organisations in south-eastern Australia towards those in remote areas who more closely resemble the romantic stereotype.

But the Indigenous identity of most Aboriginal people living in cities is not something which is invented or contrived; it is a residual and living set of relationships built on the experience of racism and social disadvantage, something quite different from that which is presented in dominant essentialist public representations. Aboriginal culture has a contemporary form that is far from being a facsimile of ancient tradition. As the social circumstances in which they find themselves change, as they are forced to adapt to the pressures which are placed on them by colonialism, the everyday significance of many inherited forms recede – connections to land, ancient rituals, forms of spirituality – and new articulations emerge. These do not represent a breach with the past or a point of disjunction. They continue to be the forms that serve to constitute Aboriginal solidarity and they are no less Indigenous culture than are corroborees, dreaming stories and body paint.

Conclusion

This book has looked at the relationship between Aboriginal people and cities and at the management of that relationship by colonial authorities. Much of what it means to be a subject and citizen of the West is embodied in cities. Cities insulate us from natural processes; they are the places where the delineation of public and private space is most marked, the division of labour most developed and the impersonal relations of the market most concentrated. The idea that civilisation obtains its most mature expression where population densities are highest is a profoundly European one. Those who inhabited the land before 1788 did not acknowledge the symbolic line between urban and rural, city and bush, and their presence in the streets of cities and towns confronted the refined pretensions of the colonisers. One of the challenges faced by those involved in Indigenous affairs was how to deal with the presence of Aboriginal people in densely settled places.

The history of the relationship of Aboriginal people to the urban sphere is one of resistance and defiance. In early colonial times many of those who came to live in towns were refugees from wars of conquest. When they no longer had access to the food sources on their land they moved to the cities and towns to gather the crumbs from the whitefella's table. This exposed them to both pity and scorn and prompted the state to instigate a system of spatial management in part aimed at safeguarding the space of civilisation. This system was never completely successful. Reserves were created ostensibly to encourage Aboriginal people to rediscover something of the Arcadian existence that romantics imagined that they had practised before the arrival of Europeans. But they were also places in which to sequester those deemed too savage for town life and those who had been removed from their traditional lands.

Later, in the twentieth century, they became places where authorities claimed to be cultivating 'civility'. The New South Wales Aborigines Welfare Board tried to convince the public that reserves were places of gentle tutelage. They were never this. While the smiling teeth in the black-and-white photos of *Dawn* magazine communicated the message that all was well in Aboriginal affairs, thousands of young Aboriginal people were making for the inner-city areas, to escape the clutches of the mission managers and police. The state and most conventional anthropologists averted their gaze. They continued to focus on the 'real Aborigines', and pretended that urban Kooris were on the road to assimilation. They were not. They formed new solidarities with people from other lands and built a new collective culture. But their presence excited the moral opprobrium of many of their neighbours and of the mainstream media and sparked the sort of biological racism characteristic of the nineteenth century.

In the late 1960s the state granted Indigenous Australians more extensive citizenship rights and also officially acknowledged that they remained Aboriginal even after they had moved to the cities. They were neither out of place, nor were they en route towards cultural uniformity with their non-Indigenous neighbours. The Housing for Aborigines (HFA) programme was part of this break with the past. Politicians described it as a liberal and integrationist break with the past. Yet the racism routinely practised by the petty officials of the Housing Commission belied this vision of the Aboriginal citizen welcomed into the social mainstream. Most of those who took up the tenancies experienced radical material improvements in their lives but most also believed that their treatment by the Housing Commission had much in common with their treatment by the Welfare Board. At an everyday level there was more continuity than rupture in their dealings with the state.

So there has always been a gulf between the humane and progressivist rhetoric that characterises the proclamations of policies and the everyday effects and practice of Indigenous affairs. In the late-eighteenth and early-nineteenth centuries, despite the official affirmations that Aboriginal people were subjects of the Crown and entitled to protection under British law, the state turned a blind eye to the murders and rapes. Although the authorities claimed they were places of protection and welfare, in fact government reserves were places of social engineering and the inculcation of shame. While politicians claimed that the dissolution of the Welfare Boards would herald a brave new world for Aboriginal people, they continued to suffer treatment by public officials and neighbours in the new suburban estates. It is little wonder that many Aboriginal people have viewed the politics of Reconciliation with some scepticism. They know from bitter experience that such things can be little more than window dressing and that very little will change in everyday life.

Aboriginal city dwellers often articulate primordial and essentialist definitions of their collective identity. This seems paradoxical because they are far removed in time and space from their traditions. Yet many of those who have migrated from the Third or Developing Worlds to the West cling to their ethnic traditions and morality, long after these have been abandoned in their homelands. In response to a feeling of being overwhelmed by modern metropolitan culture they are apt to embrace fierce traditionalism and/or fundamentalism. This is especially so where they occupy marginal social positions in the adopted country. In view of this, the tendency of Indigenous people in cities to construct Aboriginality in essentialist terms is not surprising. Like most migrants, they are among the poorest and least powerful people. Traditional Indigenous symbols appear to confer greater legitimacy on their claims to Aboriginality, and allow them to avoid being caught in the dangerous liminal cultural territory of the fringe dweller. However, this strategic essentialism has drawbacks as well as benefits. It allows urban Aboriginal people to refer to symbols and motifs that are broadly familiar to non-Indigenous Australians, many of whom now hold Indigenous traditional culture in high regard. But in doing so they suggest that Aboriginality occupies a completely separate sphere, not sufficiently recognising the hybridising effects of colonialism.

The dangers of the idea of an essential Aboriginality are exposed through the politics of self-determination. At a certain point in history the act of resisting was associated with a process of separating and homogenising. It was important to assert the existence of a pan-Aboriginal public in order for Indigenous people to wrest control of their affairs from the state. But it is foolhardy to ignore the lines of difference and social distinction within the

Aboriginal social order that can make the operation of self-determination problematic. These differences – of geography and class for example – are a product of the histories of colonialism and are often concealed by the language and politics of community. Ironically the narratives associated with self-determination often construct the idea of Indigenous social order in similar terms to nineteenth-century humanist advocates of protection. The challenge for both black and white Australia is to address contemporary colonial relations and confront the social problems of Aboriginal people without recourse to romantic ideas of Aboriginality.

Notes

Chapter 1
Colonial Geographies in Early New South Wales

1 New South Wales Parliamentary Debates, First Series Session 1885–1886, House of Assembly 4 May 1886, p. 1644.

2 'New South Wales Aborigines Protection Board Report 1903', in *New South Wales Parliamentary Papers*, 1904, vol. 66, pt. 2, p. 73.

3 This was probably a description of Bungaree, a man from the Sydney region who had accompanied Matthew Flinders on voyages, and later became a familiar character in the town. He was known, according to Reece, as a 'celebrated mimic of prominent personalities and was always easily recognizable in the cocked hat and military uniform given to him by various governors' (Reece 1974, p. 6).

Chapter 2
Uplifting Fantasies: Modernism and the Quest for Aboriginal Advancement

1 1500 children were removed from their families between 1912 and 1938 (Goodall 1995, p. 80).

2 I will use the term 'reserve' to refer to all such places although reserves with managers were usually referred to as 'stations' and the term mission was more commonly used by Aboriginal people themselves despite the fact that churches were not involved in administering such places at this time.

3 For a more detailed analysis of the politics of Aboriginal housing in regional areas in this period see Goodall 1995.

4 A meeting of Commonwealth and state ministers with responsibilities for Aboriginal affairs was held in Canberra in 1951 (although not all states were represented) and made the following statement: *The Commonwealth and the States, having assimilation as their object of native welfare measures, desire to see all persons born in Australia enjoying full citizenship. We recognise that some of the barriers against the enjoyment of all the privileges of citizenship today are not legal but social barriers. These citizens will only enjoy the privileges of citizenship if they can live and work as accepted members of the community* (cited in Gale 1964, pp. 125–126).

5 Letter sent to A Max Allen, Director of Reconstruction and Development in Sydney. Commonwealth Archives CP 43/1 Bundle 46/1944/428. Replies also included in same file.

6 When the New South Wales Housing Commission took over responsibility for most Aboriginal housing in the late sixties it adopted a 'salt and pepper' policy of suburban dispersal, rather than following the strategy earlier favoured by Elkin.

7 This observation is based on discussions over the last decade with my Aboriginal students at the University of Western Sydney.

8 Ibid.

9 Commonwealth Archives CP 43/1 Bundle 46/1944/428.

10 Described in the evidence provided by Kingsmill to the Joint Parliamentary Committee, 1967, p. 4.

11 There were exceptions to this. Greg Davis was a Dhanghaddi man who sought to rent a house in Nambucca Heads in 1958. Although he was employed his efforts were frustrated after discriminatory treatment by real-estate agents and prospective neighbours. After some adverse publicity in the metropolitan press, he overcame this hostility with the assistance of some local sympathetic whites.

12 After the Joint Parliamentary Committee had recommended the mainstreaming of Aboriginal housing but before the Board's responsibility had been passed over to the Housing Commission.

13 New migrants to Australia would also enjoy 'rights' and incur 'obligations' when they settled. Not for the first time Aboriginal policy matched that which was being applied to other groups.

Chapter 3
Profane Presence: Urbanisation and Pan-Aboriginality

1 Some of these people had sought Exemption Certificates, most had not.

2 Even after they were included, the reluctance of Aboriginal people to report information to governments, coupled with the low literacy rates, has meant that census data has never been particularly reliable.

3 This disparity is partly explained by the high mortality rates amongst Aboriginal people.

4 Men were often away from their wives doing seasonal work in the bush.

5. This had changed little by 1908 when the central city population density of Sydney was 38.3 as compared with 13.4 for Melbourne and 12.9 for Perth. [Figures from New South Wales Parliamentary Papers 1909, vol. 5 XXIV]

6 The *Bulletin*, 'The Model Suburb Notion' October 20 1888, p. 18.

7 The *Bulletin* 3 March 1888, p. 5.

8 A later study by Eckermann (1977) noted there was a convergence in values between Aboriginal city dwellers and the white working class nevertheless, and enduring cultural distinctiveness.

9 *Weekend Australian*, 17–18 February 1990; *Sydney Morning Herald*, 15 September 1997.

10 'The Block', broadcast 12 May 1997, producer Liz Jackson.

11 These were revealed by ethnographies conducted in cities other than Sydney but we can safely infer that similar cleavages also existed in Sydney.

Chapter 4
Suburban Dreaming

1 These files, long submerged in the vaults of the New South Wales State Records Office, have now been indexed to permit their use in Aboriginal family history research.

2 New South Wales State Government Archives Files of the Housing Commission. Housing For Aborigines files were termed Special Tenancy (ST) Files.

3 New South Wales Legislative Assembly Debates 18 February 1969 pp. 3721–3744.

4 The 1967 federal election determined that the Commonwealth Government could assume the responsibility for legislating in the area of Aboriginal affairs. The constitutional situation was changed such that the Housing Commission, in administering the HFA scheme, was acting as an agent for the federal not the state government.

5 The landmark Henderson Commission into Poverty in Australia highlighted the difficulties that many Aboriginal people had with the application process. The report noted that Housing Commission application procedures had long been:

> *geared to middle class white society and Aboriginals brought up in humpies or who are not very skilled at understanding and answering the officialese of government application forms can hardly avoid difficulties* (Henderson 1975, p264).

6 Rental for HFA dwellings was initially set at an economic rent or 15 per cent of gross income (increased to 20 per cent in the mid 1970s) whichever was the lesser. Applicants for housing could nominate whether they wished to be included on the HFA waiting list, the mainstream list or both. Most opted for both but their chances of obtaining an HFA place sooner were greater. Whichever option they chose, they underwent a standard Housing Commission assessment process.

7 The 1967 Joint Parliamentary committee had recommended that the Housing Commission take responsibility for the housing stock located on reserves for future Aboriginal housing provision. When the HFA programme was first established the Housing Commission undertook a gradual process of transferring reserve housing to a newly formed body, the Aboriginal Lands Trust.

8 This was probably an underestimate in view of the poor rates of distribution and completion of census forms amongst such households.

9 The remainder of this chapter draws heavily on qualitative data taken from the HFA Special Tenancy Files of the New South Wales Housing Commission

10 It had been part of the very limited town housing stock inherited from the AWB in 1969.

11 Interviewed 17 August 1998

12 For a recent profile of the problems of this area, see *Sydney Morning Herald*, 7–8 January 2006, p. 17.

13 Beasley observed of those living in Commission houses in the 1960s, prior to the introduction of HFA, that households contained fewer people and that there were more nuclear family households than was the case among those living in private rental accommodation in the inner city (Beasley 1970, p. 148). This was clearly a consequence of the pressures that were placed on tenants by the Housing Commission at the time.

14 Housing Commission Tenancy Files ST 2374 Box 10/41266
15 ST 1997 Box 14/1455

Chapter 5
Unsettling Narratives

1 All names in this chapter are fictitious.
2 In this sense she is unusual among urban Aboriginal people, many of whom articulate a traditional/ ancient culture version of their collective identities notwithstanding their contemporary life situations. This will be explored in more depth in the next chapter.

Chapter 6
Contemporary Aboriginalities

1 I am concerned in this chapter with culture in the anthropological sense, as a whole way of life and in particular with the everyday expressions of Aboriginality, rather than specifically with Indigenous creative cultural production in the arts and media.

Bibliography

General References

Aboriginal Housing Company, *Pemulwuy Reconstruction Project* (www.ahc.org.au), 2003

A.Ahmad, 'The Politics of Literary Postcoloniality' *Race and Class*, 1995, 36, 1–20

I. Anderson, 'Flag of Convenience' *The Independent Monthly*, February 1995, 44–45

I. Anderson, 'Reclaiming Tru-ger-nan-ner: Decolonising the Symbol' in P. Van Toorn, D. English (eds) *Speaking Positions: Aboriginality Gender and Ethnicity in Australian Cultural Studies*, Melbourne: Department of Humanities, Victoria University of Technology, 1995

K. Anderson, 'Constructing Geographies: Race, Place and the making of Sydney's Aboriginal Redfern' in P. Jackson and J. Penrose (eds), *Constructions of Race, Place and Nation*, London: UCL Press, 1993

K. Anderson, 'Place narratives and the origins of inner Sydney's Aboriginal Settlement 1972–73', *Journal of Historical Geography*, 1993a, 314–335

K. Anderson, 'Savagery and Urbanity: Struggles over Aboriginal Housing in Redfern' in P. Read, *Settlement. A History of Australian Indigenous Housing*, Canberra: Aboriginal Studies Press, 2000

ANZ Bank, *Australian Housing Survey*, Melbourne: ANZ, 1958

V. Attenbrow, *Sydney's Aboriginal Past. Investigating the Archaeological and Historical Records*, Sydney: UNSW Press, 2002

B. Attwood, 'Portrait of an Aboriginal as an Artist: Sally Morgan and the Construction of Aboriginality' in *Australian Historical Studies*, 1992, 25/9, 309–18

B. Attwood and A. Markus, *The 1967 referendum, or, When Aborigines didn't get the vote*, Canberra: Aboriginal Studies Press, 1997

M. Bakhtin, 'Social Heteroglossia' in P. Morris (ed.), *The Bakhtin Reader*, London: Edward Arnold, 1994

F. Barnett, *The Unsuspected Slums*, Melbourne: Herald Press, 1933

F. Barnett and W. Burt, *Housing the Australian Nation*, Melbourne: Left Book Club of Victoria, 1942

D. Barwick, 'Economic Absorption Without Assimilation The Case of Some Melbourne Part-Aboriginal Families', *Oceania*, 1962, 23, 18–23

D. Barwick, 'Writing Aboriginal History – Comments on a book and its reviewers' *Canberra Anthropology*, 1981, 4, 74–85

P. Beasley, 'The Aboriginal Household in Sydney', in R. Taft, J. Dawson, J. and P. Beasley (eds), *Attitudes and Social Conditions: Aborigines in Australian Society 2*, Canberra: Australian National University Press, 1970

J. Beckett, 'Aborigines, Alcohol and Assimilation', M. Reay (ed.) *Aborigines Now: New Perspectives in the Study of Aboriginal Communities*, Sydney: Angus and Robertson, 1964
J. Beckett, 'Kinship, Mobility and Community Among Part-Aborigines in Rural Australia' *International Journal of Comparative Sociology*, 1965, 6, 7–23
J. Beckett, 'A study of the mixed-blood Aboriginal minority in pastoral West of New South Wales', Australian National University: Master of Arts dissertation 1963
D. Bell, *Daughters of the Dreaming*, Melbourne: McPhee Gribble, 1983
J. Bell, 'Some Demographic and Cultural Characteristics of the La Perouse Aborigines' *Mankind*, 1961, 5, 425–38
K. Bell, 'The State Housing Commission and Aboriginal Housing 1959' *Studies in Western Australian History*, 1989, 10
C. Berndt, 'Mateship or Success: An Assimilation Dilemma', *Oceania*, 1962, 32, 16–33
C. Berndt and R. Berndt, *The First Australians*, Sydney: Ure Smith, 1952
C. Berndt and R. Berndt *From Black to White in South Australia* Melbourne: Cheshire, 1951
H. Bhabha, 'Signs Taken for Wonders: Questions of Ambivalence and Authority Under a Tree Outside Delhi', *Critical Inquiry*, 1985, 12/1 144–65
H. Bhabha, *The Location of Culture*, London: Routledge, 1994
T. Birch, 'Nothing has changed': the making and unmaking of Koori culture' in M. Grossman (ed.) *Blacklines: contemporary critical writing by Indigenous Australians* Carlton: Melbourne University Press, 2003
G. Bottomley, 'Ethnicity, Race and Nationalism in Australia: Some Critical Perspectives' *Australian Journal of Social Issues* 1988, 23/3, 169–83
A. Brah 'Difference, Diversity and Differentiation' in J. Donald and A. Rattansi (eds) *'Race', Culture and Difference*, London: Sage, 1992
T. Brennan, *At home in the world: cosmopolitanism now*, Cambridge, Mass.: Harvard University Press, 1997
B. Bridges, 'The Colonisation of Australia: a note in Defence of the Stanner Thesis' *Teaching History*, 1977, 11/3, 40–44
K. Brindle, 'The Urban Aboriginal in NSW', *New Dawn*, August 1970
P. Brock, *Women, rites and sites: Aboriginal women's cultural knowledge*, Sydney: Allen & Unwin, 1989
J. Brook and J. Kohen, *The Parramatta Native Institution and the Black Town: A History*, Sydney: University of New South Wales Press, 1991
L. Bryson and S. Thompson, *An Australian Newtown*, Ringwood: Penguin, 1972
T. Buggy and J. Cates *Race Relations in Colonial Australia* Melbourne: Thomas Nelson, 1982
M. Burgmann, 'Black sisterhood: the situation of urban Aboriginal women and their relationship to the white women's movement', *Politics*, 1982, 17/2, 23–37
I. Burnley, *Atlas of the Australian People– 1991 Census. New South Wales*, Canberra: Australian Government Publishing Service, 1996
D. Byrne, 'Deep Nation: Australia's acquisition of an indigenous past', *Aboriginal History*, 1996, 20: 82–107
M. Calley, 'Economic Life of Mixed Blood Communities in Northern New South Wales'. *Oceania* 1956, 26/3 200–213.
A. Chase, 'Empty Vessels and Loud Noises; views about Aboriginality today', *Social Alternatives*, 1981, 2/2, 23–27
J. Clifford, *The Predicament of Culture. Twentieth Century Ethnography, Literature and Art*, Cambridge, Mass.: Harvard University Press, 1988
J. Clifford and G. Marcus, *Writing Culture: The poetics and the politics of ethnography*, Berkely: University of California Press, 1986
J. Collman, *Fringe Dwellers and Welfare: The Aboriginal Response to Bureaucracy*, Brisbane: University of Queensland Press, 1988

G. Cowlishaw 'Australian Aboriginal Studies: The Anthropologists' Accounts' M. de Lepervanche and G. Bottomley (eds) *The Cultural Construction of Race*, Sydney: Sydney Association for Studies in Society and Culture, 1988
G. Cowlishaw, *Black, White or Brindle. Race in Rural Australia*, Melbourne: Cambridge Univerity Press, 1988a
G. Cowlishaw, 'Introduction: Representing Racial Issues' *Oceania* 1993, 63/3 183–94
G. Cowlishaw, 'Studying Aborigines: Changing Canons in Anthropology and History' in B. Attwood, B. and J. Arnold (eds) *Power, Knowledge and Aborigines*, Bundoora: La Trobe University Press, 1992
G. Cowlishaw, *Blackfellas, Whitfellas and the hidden injuries of race*, Sydney: Allen and Unwin, 2004
C. Critcher, 'Sociology, Cultural Studies and the Postwar Working Class' in J. Clarke, C. Critcher, and R. Johnson (eds) *Working Class Culture. Studies in History and Theory*, London: Hutchinson, 1979
A. Curthoys, *Freedom Ride: A Freedom Rider Remembers*, Sydney: Allen and Unwin, 2002
F. Debenham (ed.), *The Voyage of Captain Bellinghausen to the Antarctic Seas 1819–21*, London: Hakluyt Society, 1945
M. Dodson, 'The Wentworth Lecture The end in the beginning: re(de)finding Aboriginality' *Australian Aboriginal Studies*, 1994, 1, 2–13
A. Earl, *A narrative of nine month' residence in New Zealand in 1827; together with a journal of residence in Tristan D'Acunha, and island situated between South America and the Cape of Good Hope*, London: Longman, 1832
A. Eckermann, 'Group Organisation and Identity Within an Urban Aboriginal Community' in R. Berndt *Aborigines and Change: Australia in the '70s*, New Jersey: Humanities Press, 1977
C. Edwards and P. Read, *The Lost Children*, Sydney: Doubleday, 1989
A. Elkin, *Citizenship for Aborigines. A National Aboriginal Policy*, Sydney: Australian Publishing Company, 1944
A. Elkin, *The Australian Aborigines: how to understand them*, Sydney: Angus and Robertson, 1938
F. Fanon, *The Wretched of the Earth*, New York: Random House, 1967
B. Field, *Geographical Memoirs on New South Wales*, London: John Murray, 1825
R. Fink, 'The Caste Barrier – An Obstacle to the Assimilation of Part-Aborigines in North-West New South Wales', *Oceania*, 1957, 28/2, 100–110
J. Fletcher, *Clean, clad and courteous: A history of Aboriginal school education in New South Wales*, Sydney: Southwood Press, 1989
M. Franklin, *Assimilation in Action. The Armidale Story*, Armidale: University of New England Press, 1995
J. Friedman, *Cultural identity and global process*, London: Sage, 1994
F. Gale, A Study of Assimilation. Part-Aborigines in South Australia (PhD thesis, University of Adelaide, 1964)
F. Gale, *Urban Aborigines*, Canberra: Australian National University Press, 1972
A. Gargett, 'A Critical Media Analysis of the Redfern Riot', *Indigenous Law Bulletin*, 2005 6/10, 8–11
K. Gelder and J. Jacobs, *Uncanny Australia: sacredness and identity in a postcolonial nation*, Carlton: Melbourne University Press, 1998
A. Giddens, *The Consequences of Modernity*, Cambridge: Polity, 1990
K. Gilbert, *Living Black: blacks talk to Kevin Gilbert*, Ringwood: Penguin, 1977
P. Gilroy, 'Problems in anti-racist strategy', London: Runnymede Lecture, 23 July 1987
P. Gilroy, *There Ain't No Black in the Union Jack*, London: Hutchinson, 1987
H. Goodall, 'Assimilation Begins at Home: The State and Aboriginal women's work as mothers in New South Wales, 1900s to 1960s' in A. McGrath, K. Saunders and

J. Huggins (eds) *Aboriginal Workers*, Sydney: Australian Society for the Study of Labour History, 1995

H. Goodall, *Invasion to embassy: land in Aboriginal politics in New South Wales, 1770–1972*, St Leonards, NSW: Allen & Unwin in association with Black Books, 1996

A. Gramsci, *Selections from Prison Notebooks*, London: Lawrence and Wishart, 1971

G. Gray, 'AP Elkin and Aboriginal Advancement' in N. Petersen, and W. Sanders (eds), *Citizenship and Indigenous Australians. Changing Conceptions and Possibilities*, Melbourne: Cambridge University Press, 1998

A. Greig, *The Stuff Dreams are Made Of: Housing Provision in Australia 1945–60*, Melbourne: Melbourne University Press, 1995

S. Hall, 'New Ethnicities' in J. Donald and A. Rattansi (eds), *'Race', Culture and Difference*, London: Sage, 1992

S. Hall, 'The West and the Rest: Discourse and Power' in S. Hall and B. Gieben (eds), *Formations of Modernity*, London: Polity, 1992a

S. Hall, 'When Was 'The Post-Colonial'? Thinking at the Limit' in I. Chambers and L. Curti (eds) *The Post-Colonial Question*, London: Routledge, 1996

A. Hamilton, 'Fear and Desire – Aborigines, Asians and the National Imaginary', *Australian Cultural History*, 1990, 9, 16–36

J. Hartley, 'Black, White ... and Red? The Redfern All Blacks Rugby League Club in the Early 1960s', in *Labour History* (Australia) November 2002, 83, 149–72

P. Hasluck, *Shades of Darkness. Aboriginal Affairs, 1925–65*, Melbourne: Melbourne University Press, 1988

C. Healy, *From the ruins of colonialism : history as social memory*, Cambridge: Cambridge University Press, 1997

R. Henderson, *Commission of Enquiry into Poverty. First Main Report April 1975*, Canberra: Australian Government Publishing Service, 1975

M. Hinkson, *Aboriginal Sydney: A guide to important places of the past and present*, Canberra: Aboriginal Studies Press, 2001

B. Hodge and V. Mishra *Dark Side of the Dream*, Sydney: Allen and Unwin, 1991

R. Hoggart, *The Uses of Literacy*, Harmondsworth: Penguin, 1958

D. Hollinsworth, 'Discourses on Aboriginality and the Politics of Identity in Urban Australia' *Oceania* 1992, 63, 137–71

R. Hughes, *The Fatal Shore. The Epic of Australia's Founding*, New York: Vintage, 1988

Human Rights and Equal Opportunity Commission *Bringing them home: report of the National Inquiry into the Separation of Aboriginal and Torres Strait Islander Children from their Families*, Sydney : Human Rights and Equal Opportunity Commission 1997

J. Inglis, 'Aborigines in Adelaide' *Polynesian Society Journal*, 1961, 70/2, 200–218

R. Johnson, G. McLennan, B. Schwarz and D. Sutton (eds) *Making Histories. Studies in history-writing and politics* London: Hutchinson, 1982

D. Jones, and J. Hill-Burnett, 'The Political Context of Ethnogenesis: An Australian Example' in M. Howard (ed.), *Aboriginal Power in Australian Society*, St Lucia: University of Queensland Press, 1992

R. Jones, 'The housing need of indigenous Australians', 94. Australian National University Centre for Aboriginal Economic Policy Research, Research Monographs, 1991

M. Kamien, *The Dark People of Bourke. A Study in Planned Social Change*, New Jersey: Humanities Press, 1978

I. Keen, *Being black : Aboriginal cultures in 'settled' Australia*, Canberra: Aboriginal Studies Press, 1988

C. Kelly, 'The Reaction of White Groups in Country Towns of New South Wales to Aborigines'. *Social Horizons* 1943, 34–40

J. Kohen, *The Darug and Their Neighbours: The Traditional Aboriginal Owners of the Sydney Region*, Sydney: Blacktown and District Historical Society, 1993

J. Kohen 'First and Last People: Aboriginal Sydney' in J. Connell (ed.). *Sydney the emergence of a global city*, Melbourne: Oxford University Press, 2000
R. Langford, *Don't Take Your Love to Town*, Ringwood: Penguin, 1988
M. Langton, 'Urbanising Aborigines. The Social Scientists' Great Deception' *Social Alternatives*, 1981, 2/2, 16–22
M. Langton, '*Well I Heard it on the Radio and I Saw it on the Television' An Essay for the Australian Film Commission on the Politics and Aesthetics of Film Making by and about Aboriginal people and things*, Sydney: Australian Film Commission, 1993
A. Lattas, 'Essentialism, Memory and Resistance: Aboriginality and the Politics of Authenticity' *Oceania* 1993, 63/3, 240–67
A Lattas, 'Wiping the Blood Off Aboriginality: The Politics of Aboriginal Embodiment in Contemporary Intellectual Debate', *Oceania*, 63/2, 160–64
C. Levi-Strauss, *The Raw and The Cooked*, London: Cape, 1970
C. Levi Strauss, *Tristes Tropiques*, Harmondsworth: Penguin, 1976
J. Lickiss, 'Aboriginal Children in Sydney. The Socio Economic Environment' in *Oceania*, 1971, 16/3, 201–28
L. Lippmann, *Words or Blows. Racial Attitudes in Australia*, Ringwood: Penguin, 1973
C. Liston, *Campbelltown The Bicentennial History*, Sydney: Allen and Unwin, 1988
J. Long, *Aboriginal Settlements: A Survey of Institutional Communities in Eastern Australia*, Canberra: Institute of Aboriginal Studies, 1970
F. Lovejoy, 'Costing the Aboriginal housing problem'. *The Australian Quarterly*, 1971, 43/1, 79–90
I. MacKay, 'Housing for Aborigines in New South Wales', *Architecture in Australia*, 1968
G. Marcus and M. Fisher, *Anthropology as Cultural Critique: An Experimental Moment in the Human Sciences*, Chicago: University of Chicago Press, 1986
J. Marcus, 'Introduction: Anthropology, Culture and Post-modernity', *Social Analysis*, 1990, 27
A. Mayne, *The Imagined Slum: Newspaper Representation in Three Cities*, Leicester: Leicester University Press, 1993
J. McCorquodale, 'Administrative Identity: Legislative, Judicial and Administrative Definitions', *Australian Aboriginal Studies*, 1997, 2, 24–35
G. McDonald, 'Contextualising Cultural Continuities in New South Wales' in G. Morgan (ed.) *Urban Life, Urban Culture– Aboriginal Indigenous Experiences* Conference Proceedings: University of Western Sydney, 1998
G. McDonald, 'A Wiradjuri Fight Story' in I. Keen (ed.), *Being Black*, Canberra: Aboriginal Studies Press, 1988
A. McGrath, *Born in the Cattle*, Sydney: Allen and Unwin, 1987
R. McGregor *Imagined Destinies. Aboriginal Australians and the Doomed Race Theory, 1880–1939*, Melbourne: Melbourne University Press, 1997
S. McIntyre, *A Concise History of Australia*, Melbourne: Melbourne University Press, 1999
I. McLeod, *Shade and Shelter: The Story of Aboriginal Family Resettlement*, Milton: Jacaranda, 1982
F. Merlan, *Caging the Rainbow: Places, Politics and Aborigines in a North Australian Town*, Honolulu: University of Hawai'i Press, 1998
S. Meucke, *Textual Spaces Aboriginality and Cultural Studies*, Sydney: University of New South Wales Press, 1992
E. Michaels, *The Aboriginal Invention of Television in Central Australia 1982–86*, Canberra: Australian Institute of Aboriginal Studies, 1986
J. Miller, *Koori: A Will to Win. The Heroic Resistance, Survival and Triumph of Black Australia*, Sydney: Angus and Robertson, 1988

I. Mitchell, Aborigines on the Move: Personal adjustment in the Resettlement of Aboriginal Families: A Psychological Study (PhD dissertation, University of Sydney, 1978)
G. Morgan, 'The Bulletin and the Larrikin Moral Panic in Late Nineteenth Century Sydney', *Media International Australia*, 1997, 85, 17–23
G. Morgan, 'The Moral Surveillance of Aboriginal Applicants for Public Housing in New South Wales in the 1970s' in *Australian Aboriginal Studies*, 1999, 2, 3–14
G. Morgan, 'Assimilation and Resistance: Housing Indigenous Australians in the 1970s', *Journal of Sociology*, 2000, 36/3, 187–204
G. Morgan, 'The Urban Renewal of Prejudice', *Australian Financial Review*, 5 March 2004, 4–5
S. Morgan, *My Place*, Fremantle: Fremantle Arts Centre Press, 1987
B. Morris, 'Making Histories/Living History' *Social Analysis*, 1995, 27, 83–92
B. Parry, 'Problems in Current Theories of Colonial Discourse' in B. Ashcroft, G. Griffiths, G. & H. Tiffin (eds), *The Post-Colonial Studies Reader*, London: Routledge, 1995
L. Parry, 'The Convict Road: Frontier, Boundary and Mobility' paper presented at Australian Cultural Studies Association conference, December 1994
M. Peel, *Good times, hard times : the past and the future in Elizabeth* , Melbourne: Melbourne University Press, 1995
D. Plater, 'Aboriginal people and 'community' in the Leichhardt municipality' in S. Fitzgerald and G. Wotherspoon (eds), *Minorities. Cultural Diversity in Sydney*, Sydney: State Library of NSW Press, 1995
Popular Memory Group 'Popular Memory: Theory, Politics, Method' in R .Johnson, G. McLennan, B. Schwarz and D. Sutton (eds) *Making Histories. Studies in history-writing and politics*. London: Hutchinson, 1992
E. Povinelli, *The Cunning of Recognition: Indigenous Alterities and the Making of Australian Multiculturalism*, Durham, North Carolina: Duke University Press, 2002
A. Rattansi, 'Post-Colonialism and its Discontents' *Economy and Society*, 1997, 26, 480–500
P. Read, and C. Edwards, *The Lost children: thirteen Australians taken from their Aboriginal families tell of the struggle to find their natural parents*, Sydney: Doubleday, 1989
P. Read, *A hundred years war: the Wiradjuri people and the state*, Sydney : Australian National University Press, 1988.
P. Read, *Settlement. A History of Australian Indigenous Housing*, Canberra: Aboriginal Studies Press, 2000
M. Reay and G. Stiltington, 'Class and Status in a Mixed-Blood Community', *Oceania*, 1948, 18
R. Reece, *Aborigines and Colonists. Aborigines and Colonial Society in New South Wales in the 1830s and 1840s*, Sydney: Sydney University Press, 1974
B. Reece, 'Inventing Aborigines' *Aboriginal History*, 1987 11/1, 14–23
H. Reynolds, *Frontier*, Sydney: Allen and Unwin, 1987
H. Reynolds, *The Law of the Land*, Sydney: Allen and Unwin, 1987a
H. Reynolds, *The Other Side of the Frontier. Aboriginal Resistance to the European Invasion of Australia*, Ringwood: Penguin, 1982
H. Reynolds, *With the White People: The crucial role of Aborigines in the exploration and development of Australia*, Ringwood: Penguin, 1990
S. Rintoul, *The Wailing. A National Black Oral History*, Melbourne: Heinemann, 1993
H. Ross, *Just for living: Aboriginal perceptions of housing in northwest for the* , Canberra: Australian Aboriginal Studies Press, 1987
K. Ross, 'Population Issues, Indigenous Australians', 99, Canberra, Australian Bureau of Statistics Occasional Papers 1999
C. Rowley, 'Social Science Research Council Aboriginals Project', Social Science Research Council, n.d.

C. Rowley, *The destruction of Aboriginal society*, Ringwood: Penguin 1972a
C. Rowley, *Outcasts in White Australia: Aboriginal Policy and Practice* , Canberra: Australian National University Press, 1971
C. Rowley, *The Remote Aborigines*, Harmondsworth: Penguin, 1972
T. Rowse, *After Mabo: interpreting indigenous traditions*, Carlton.: Melbourne University Press, 1993
T. Rowse, 'Are we All Blow Ins. A Review of Black, White of Brindle: Race in Rural Australia', *Oceania*, 1990, 61/2, 185–92
T. Rowse, 'Rethinking Aboriginal "Resistance": The Community Development Employment (CEPD) Program', *Oceania*, 1993, 63, 268–86
T. Rowse, 'Indigenous Citizenship and Self Determination: The Problem of Shared Responsibility' in N. Peterson and W. Sanders (eds) *Citizenship and Indigenous Australians; Changing Conceptions and Possibilities* Melbourne: Cambridge University Press, 1998
T. Rowse, 'The Principles of Aboriginal Pragmatism' in M. Goot, and T. Rowse (eds) *Make a Better Offer– The Politics of Mabo*, Sydney: Pluto Press, 1994
T. Rowse, *Remote possibilities : the Aboriginal domain and the administrative imagination*, Darwin: North Australia Research Unit, Australian National University, 1992
T. Rowse, 'Strehlow's Strap: Functionalism and Historicism in Colonial Ethnography' in B. Attwood and J. Arnold (eds) *Power, Knowledge and Aborigines*, Melbourne: La Trobe University Press, 1992
T. Rowse, *White Flour, White Power. From Rations to Citizenship in Central Australia*, Melbourne: Cambridge University Press, 1998
T. Rowse, *Obliged to be Difficult: Nugget Coombs' Legacy in Indigenous Affairs*, Cambridge: Cambridge University Press, 2000
J. Sabbioni, 'Aboriginal Women's Narratives – Reconstructing Identities', *Australian Historical Studies*, 1996, 106, 72–78
M. Sahlins, Ethnographic Experience and Sentimental Pessimism: Why Culture is Not a Disappearing Object, in L. Daston (ed.), *Biographies of Scientific Objects*, Chicago: University of Chicago Press, 2000
E. Said, *Orientalism*, Harmondsworth: Penguin, 1985
R. Sandall, *The Culture Cult : designer tribalism and other essays*, Roger Sandall, Boulder: Westview Press, 2001
W. Scott, A report to the Minister for Youth and Community Services, Sydney, 1973
S. Slemon, 'The Scramble for Post Colonialism' in B. Ashcroft, G. Griffiths and H. Tiffin (eds), *The Post-Colonial Studies Reader*, London: Routledge, 1995
H. Smith and E. Biddle, *Look forward, not back: Aborigines in metropolitan Brisbane 1965–1966*, Canberra: Australian National University Press, 1970
C. Spark, 'Documenting Redfern: Representing Home and Aboriginality on The Block' *Continuum: Journal of Media and Cultural Studies*, 2003, 17/1, 33–50
P. Spearritt, 'The Australian Slum Stigma' *Australian and New Zealand Journal of Sociology* 1973, 9/2, 41–45
G. Spivak, 'Subaltern Studies: Deconstructing Historiography' in R. Guha and . Spivak (eds), *Selected Subaltern Studies*, Oxford: Oxford University Press, 1988
W. Stanner, *White Man Got No Dreaming: Essays 1938–73*, Canberra: ANU Press, 1979
D. Suzuki and P. Knudtson, *Wisdom of the Elders*, New York: Bantam Books, 1993
R. Sykes, *Snake Cradle*, Sydney: Allen and Unwin, 1997
D. Tacey, *Edge of the Sacred– Transformation in Australia*, Melbourne: Harper Collins, 1995
L. Taksa, 'Everleigh Railway Workshop Management Plan: Moveable Items and Social History' Vol. 2, *Social and Oral History*, City West Corporation, 1996
C. Tatz and K. McConnochie, *Black Viewpoints: The Aboriginal Experience*, Sydney: ANZ Book Company, 1975

P. Taylor, *Telling it like it is. A guide to making Aboriginal and Torres Strait Islander history*, Canberra: Australian Institute of Aboriginal and Torres Strait Islander Studies, 1992

N. Thomas, *Entangled Objects Exchange, Material Culture, and Colonialism in the Pacific*, Cambridge: Harvard University Press, 1991

P. Thompson, *The Voice of the Past: Oral History*, Oxford: Oxford University Press, 1978

D. Trigger, *Whitefella Comin' Aboriginal Responses to Colonialism in northern Australia*, Cambridge: Cambridge University Press, 1992

P. Turbet, *The Aborigines of the Sydney District Before 1788*, Kenthurst: Kangaroo Press, 1989

E. Wait, The migration of people of Aboriginal ancestry to the metropolitan area and their assimilation (B.A. Hons dissertation, University of Sydney, 1950)

F. Wells, 'Taste of a Bitter Utopia', *Sydney Morning Herald*, 28 February 1966

R. Williams, *Marxism and Literature*, Oxford: Oxford University Press, 1977

A. Willis, *Illusions of Identity*, Sydney: Hale and Iremonger, 1993

E. Wilmot, *Pemulwuy: Rainbow Warrior*, Sydney: Weldon, 1987

G. Wotherspoon, *Sydney's Transport: Studies in Urban History* , Sydney: Hale and Iremonger, 1983

R. Yardi, R. & G. Stokes, 'Foundations for Reconciliation in social science: the political thought of C.D. Rowley', *Melbourne Journal of Politics*, 25, 45–66, 1998

E. Young, *Tribal Communities in Rural Areas*, Canberra: Development Studies Centre, Australian National University, 1981

E. Young, 'Aboriginal Town Dwellers in New South Wales' in E. Fisk and E. Young (eds) *Town Populations*, Canberra: Development Studies Centre, Australian National University, 1982

Government Publications

Commonwealth Department of Territories Pamphlet Series:

No. 57 *Our Aborigines*
No. 62 *Aboriginal Advancement*
No. 63 *The Aborigine and You*
No. 64 *Fringe Dwellers*
No. 65 *Australia's Aborigines*
No. 67 *Aborigines in the Community*

NSW Parliamentary Debates
NSW Parliamentary Papers
NSW Joint Committee of the Legislative Council and Legislative Assembly into Aborigines Welfare, 1967
NSW Legislative Committee on Aborigines, 1981
NSW Parliamentary Standing Committee on Social Issues 'Inquiry into issues relating to Redfern and Waterloo', Final Report 2004

Newspapers/Magazines

Bega Advocate
Bulletin
Dawn
HQ Magazine
Illustrated Sydney News
Inverell Times
McLeay Argus
Smith's Weekly
Sydney Gazette
Sydney Morning Herald
Truth

Index

B

C

D

I

J

K

L

M

N

O

P

R

S